The AMAZING AI – VENGERS

Crack the code of AI and create smarter world!

SIDDHARTH BHARGAVA

Learn Artificial Intelligence, in a fun way!

Copyright © 2024 Siddharth Bhargava

All rights reserved. No part of this publication may be reproduced, distributed, or transmitted in any form or by any means, including photocopying, recording, or other electronic or mechanical methods, without the prior written permission of the publisher, except in the case of brief quotations embodied in critical reviews and certain other noncommercial uses permitted by copyright law.

Calling all AI-Heroes

Hey AI-Newbies,

Get ready to blast off into the world of Artificial Intelligence (AI) – it's like magic, but REAL! This book is your ticket to the awesome adventures of AI. You'll meet AI and AI robots, learn how they think, and discover the incredible things they can do.

We'll understand how AI powers your phone, knows what movies you'll love, and even helps doctors save lives! We'll dive into the amazing technology behind AI, like super-smart robot brains, and see how it's changing the world.

But that's not all! We'll also talk about important stuff like teaching AI to be fair, how robots might help us in the future, and why building safe AI is so important. Get ready to be amazed, inspired, and learn how YOU can be a part of the exciting world of AI!

So, what are you waiting for? Grab your snacks, settle into your favorite reading spot, and let's embark on an AI adventure like no other!

Let the adventure begin !

Table Of Contents

Meet AI: Your New Super-Smart Friend!......................1

A History Of AI: Key Inventions For AI-Newbies!................11

The Building Blocks Of AI: How Does It Work?.....................19

The Science Behind AI: A Fun And Easy Explanation...........40

AI Is Everywhere! Even In Your Pocket!......................55

Generative AI: The Imagination Machine!................67

Large Language Models: The Word Wizards Of AI 77

Prompt Engineering: Whispering In AI's Ear!..........................88

Chain-Of-Thought (Cot) Prompting 98

AI Models: The Superheroes Of The Digital World!..............103

Model Hallucination 109

AI At Work: Helping Humans Do Amazing Things!.............115

AI And Us: Being Friends With Robots 123

AI & Jobs: Will AI Steal Our Jobs?...129

Our AI Future: Let's Build An Awesome World!....................133

Your AI Adventure Begins..136

Awesome Careers Of The Future 142

AI: Awesome... But Be Careful!..145

AI All-Stars: Meet The Companies Shaping The Future!......148

AI Superpowers In Action: Real-Life Magic! 153

Open-Source AI: The Power Of Sharing!................................156

Mini-Dictionary Of Awesome AI Words 160

Meet AI: Your New Super-Smart Friend!

What is AI? AI is like a brain for machines, only cooler

Imagine having a super-smart robot friend who can learn and do amazing things! That's kind of like Artificial Intelligence, or AI for short. It's not a real robot, but it's a special computer program that can think and learn just like you do!

And if you are thinking about what a program is, a computer program is a set of step-by-step instructions that tell a computer what to do. Just like a recipe tells you how to bake a cake, a program tells a computer how to perform tasks, from simple calculations to running complex video games.

Computers don't understand human language. They speak in a special language called code, which is made up of numbers, letters, and symbols. Programmers write code, which is then translated into a language that computers can understand. The computer follows these instructions one by one, like a chef following a recipe.

How does AI work?

Think of your brain. It learns by seeing, hearing, and experiencing things. AI works in a similar way. It uses special computer instructions to learn from information and get better at tasks over time. It's like a sponge soaking up knowledge!

What can AI do?

AI is like a superhero with many powers! It can:

- **Talk and understand you:** Have you ever chatted with Google home or Siri? That's AI understanding your words and talking back.

- **Play games:** AI can beat you at chess or even create new games! It's a super smart game partner.

- **Help you learn:** AI can create personalized study plans or even explain tricky math problems. It's your own homework helper!

- **Predict the future:** AI can tell you if it might rain tomorrow or suggest what movie you might like. It's like having your own fortune teller!

- **Drive cars:** Yes, some cars can drive themselves using AI. It's like having a robot chauffeur!

AI: Not a New Kid on the Block, but Now It's Got Superpowers!

Ever seen a superhero movie where a normal person suddenly gets incredible powers? Well, that's kind of what's happening with AI right now!

AI isn't actually a brand-new idea. It's been around for quite a while, like a kid who's always been good at math. But recently, AI has gone through a major growth spurt, and now it can do things that were once just dreams!

Here's the secret sauce behind AI's new superpowers:

1. **Brain Food (Data)**: AI needs tons of information to learn and grow, just like we need healthy snacks. Nowadays, we have more information than ever before, thanks to the internet. It's like a giant buffet for AI, helping it get super-smart!

2. **Super-Fast Brains (Computing power)**: Computers are now much faster and more powerful than ever

before. This means AI can process all that information super quickly, like a rocket speeding through space!

3. **Special Recipes (Algorithms)**: Scientists have come up with super-clever ways to teach AI how to learn and think. They're like top chefs who have discovered secret recipes to make the tastiest dishes ever!

Thanks to these three superpowers, AI can now do things like:

- **Chat** with us like a friend: Have you ever talked to Google home or Siri? That's AI!

- **Drive cars**: Some cars can even drive themselves, using AI to see and navigate the roads.

- **Create art** and music: AI can make paintings, compose songs, and even write stories!

- **Help doctors**: AI can analyze medical images to help doctors diagnose diseases faster and more accurately.

- **Predict** the **weather**: AI can look at tons of weather data to tell us if we should pack an umbrella or wear sunscreen.

So, while AI has been around for a while, it's only recently that it's become a real superhero, thanks to more information, faster computers, and better "recipes" for teaching it to learn! It's an exciting time to be a newbie to AI, because who knows what awesome things AI will be able to do in the future!

Awesome-AI Exercise Time!

AI Idea Generator:

Now, let's put on our inventor hats! Think of some ways AI could help You with your everyday life or make your dreams come true.

1. _____
   _____
   _____

2. _____
   _____
   _____

3. _____
   _____
   _____

Show and Tell:

Share your awesome AI ideas with your friends, family, or even your classmates! You can create a presentation, draw a picture, or even write a short story about your AI invention.

Who did you share your ideas with?

_____
_____
_____

The Future of AI

Who knows what amazing things AI will do in the future? Maybe robots will become our best friends or we'll have flying cars! The possibilities are endless! But remember, even though AI is super smart, it's still just a tool created by humans. And the most important thing is to use it wisely and for good.

Why is AI so awesome? It can do amazing things!

AI is super awesome! It's like having a magic wand that can do things we only dreamed of before. Let us explore some examples, how AI is making our world even more amazing:

AI is our personal helper:

- **Your own super-smart assistant:** AI helps you with your everyday tasks, like organizing your schedule, setting reminders, and even answering questions you have.

- **Making life easier:** AI can even help you with things like translating languages in real-time or suggesting the best route to take to avoid traffic.

- **Personalized recommendations:** Have you noticed how your favorite video streaming service always seems to know what movie you want to watch? That's AI at work, analyzing your preferences and making recommendations based on what you like.

AI is a game-changer:

- **Gaming to the next level:** AI is making video games more realistic and challenging. It creates smarter opponents and more immersive worlds that make you feel like you're part of the action.

- **New ways to play:** AI is also helping us create new kinds of games, like those that use augmented reality to let you interact with virtual characters in the real world.

AI is a problem solver:

- **Fighting climate change:** AI is helping scientists analyze huge amounts of data to understand how our planet is changing and  find solutions to environmental problems.

- **Finding new medicines:** AI is helping researchers discover new drugs to fight diseases like cancer and even predict outbreaks of illnesses.

- **Improving agriculture:** AI can help farmers monitor their crops, predict weather patterns, and optimize their irrigation systems to grow more food with fewer resources.

AI is an innovator:

- **New ways to create:** AI is helping artists and musicians create music, paintings, and even poems that are truly unique and sometimes even indistinguishable from human-made art.

- **Designing better products:** AI can help engineers design everything from cars to buildings, making them safer, more efficient, and more sustainable.

- **Exploring space:** AI is helping scientists analyze data from telescopes and spacecraft, leading to new discoveries about our universe.

AI's Awesome Numbers!

AI is like a playground filled with **BILLIONS** (Or more) of kids – that's how many smart AI helpers are working all around the world! They're like a giant team of super-smart friends helping us with all sorts of things.

Let's see some **examples**:

- There are over **500 self-driving cars** zooming around in cities like San Francisco, making traffic a little less crazy!

- Doctors use AI to help look at **millions of X-rays and scans** each year, finding problems super-fast, with the recommendations from AI based on past data

- Some artists use AI to create **millions** of amazing paintings and drawings, just like a magic paintbrush! Over 15 million images are created using AI every single day!

- Have you played against a computer in a game? That's **AI making the computer a tricky opponent!** AI can now beat the best human players at games like chess and Go.

- There are over **100 million smart speakers**, like Alexa or Google Home, using AI to understand what you're saying and answer your questions, like having your own personal know-it-all!

And to power all these amazing things, some supercomputers are so powerful that they can do more calculations in a second than all humans could do in thousands of years! How many math problems you could solve if you were THAT fast!

And guess what? There are so many more AI helpers being created every day! It's like a giant playground that's getting bigger and more fun all the time!

A History of AI: Key Inventions for AI-Newbies!

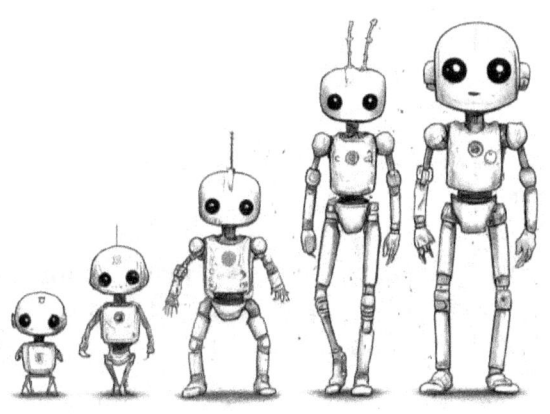

1936: The Turing Machine (The Blueprint for Computers)

- **Alan Turing:** This brilliant mathematician dreamed up a theoretical machine that could solve any problem a human could, just by following instructions. This "Turing Machine" became the foundation for modern computers and laid the groundwork for AI.

- **Key Paper:** On Computable Numbers, with an Application to the Entscheidungsproblem (1936)

1950: Computing Machinery and Intelligence (The Thinking Machine)

- **Alan Turing:** Turing asked a groundbreaking question: "Can machines think?" He proposed the Turing Test to see if a machine could convincingly imitate human intelligence.

- **Key Paper:** Computing Machinery and Intelligence (1950)

1956: The Dartmouth Workshop (The AI Summer Camp)

- **John McCarthy, Marvin Minsky, Nathaniel Rochester, and Claude Shannon:** These four visionaries organized a summer workshop at Dartmouth College, where they coined the term "Artificial Intelligence" and set the stage for AI as a field of research.

1958: The Perceptron (The First Artificial Neural Network)

- **Frank Rosenblatt:** This pioneering psychologist invented the Perceptron, a simple model of an artificial neuron. It could learn to classify simple patterns, marking a significant step in machine learning.

- **Key Paper:** The Perceptron: A Probabilistic Model for Information Storage and Organization in the Brain (1958)

1965: The Backpropagation Algorithm (The Learning Booster)

- **Arthur Bryson and Yu-Chi Ho:** They introduced backpropagation, a powerful algorithm that allows neural networks to learn from their mistakes and improve their performance. This discovery revolutionized the field of machine learning.

1969: Shakey the Robot (The First Mobile Robot)

- **Stanford Research Institute:** This groundbreaking robot could reason about its actions and navigate its environment, a major milestone in AI and robotics.

1986: NETtalk (The Talking Machine)

- **Terrence Sejnowski and Charles Rosenberg:** This neural network learned to read English text aloud, demonstrating AI's potential for language processing.

1997: Deep Blue Defeats Kasparov (The Chess Champion)

- **IBM's Deep Blue:** This supercomputer made history by defeating Garry Kasparov, the world chess champion, in a six-game match. It showcased the increasing power of AI and its ability to tackle complex problems.

2012: AlexNet (The Image Whiz)

- **Alex Krizhevsky and friends:** This deep neural network won the ImageNet competition, a major image recognition challenge, demonstrating the power of deep learning for computer vision.

- **Key Paper:** ImageNet Classification with Deep Convolutional Neural Networks (2012)

2016: AlphaGo Defeats Lee Sedol (The Go Guru)

- **DeepMind's AlphaGo:** This AI system mastered the ancient game of Go, beating a world champion and showcasing the potential of deep reinforcement learning.

2017: Transformers (The Language Wizards)

- **Google Brain Team:** This team of researchers introduced the Transformer architecture, a groundbreaking approach for processing language that revolutionized natural language processing (NLP) and led to the development of powerful language models like GPT-3.

- **Key Paper:** Attention Is All You Need (2017)

2022: ChatGPT (The Friendly Chatbot)

- **OpenAI:** This advanced language model took the world by storm with its ability to generate creative text, answer questions, and even write code. It made AI accessible to everyone and sparked excitement about the future of AI.

2023 and Beyond: The AI Revolution Continues (The Next Chapter)

- **AI is advancing at an incredible pace.** We can expect even more amazing breakthroughs in areas like healthcare, education, climate change, and space exploration. The possibilities are endless!

- **Who knows what's next?** AI is developing so quickly, who knows what amazing inventions will come next? Maybe robots that can do our chores, self-driving cars that can take us anywhere, or even AI systems that can help cure diseases. The future of AI is full of exciting possibilities!

History of AI Heroes Challenge!

Let's take a trip through time to meet the heroes of AI history and their amazing inventions! Get ready for some exciting challenges and activities:

1. Turing Test Time Machine:

Mission: You're traveling back to 1950 to meet Alan Turing, the brilliant scientist who created the Turing Test.

What to do:

Prepare some tricky questions to ask Turing's chatbot to see if you can tell it's a machine!

_____
_____
_____
_____
_____
_____
_____

Think about how you would design your own Turing Test to see if a computer is truly intelligent.

_____
_____
_____
_____
_____
_____
_____

💡 Why it matters: This helps you understand the concept of intelligence and how we can measure it in machines.

2. Deep Blue vs. Kasparov: The Ultimate Chess Match!

Mission: Witness the historic chess match between IBM's Deep Blue supercomputer and world chess champion Garry Kasparov in 1997.

What to do:

- Learn about Deep Blue's strategies and how it was able to beat Kasparov.
- Research other examples of AI beating humans at games like Go and Jeopardy!
- Think of a game that you think AI would be good at and design an AI opponent for it.

_____
_____
_____
_____
_____
_____
_____

💡 Why it matters: This helps you understand how AI has evolved and how it's now capable of tackling complex tasks that require strategy and decision-making.

Bonus Challenge:

Interview someone who works in the field of AI (a software engineer, data scientist, or even someone who uses AI tools in their work). Ask them about their experiences with AI, the challenges they face, and what they think the future of AI holds.

The Building Blocks of AI: How Does it Work?

The Recipe for Building Super-Smart AI Robots - The List!

1. **Brain Food (Data):** Just like we need healthy food to grow and learn, AI robots need a ton of information to become super smart. This information is called data, and it can be anything from pictures and words to numbers and sounds. The more  yummy data they eat, the smarter they get!

2. **Robot Recipes (Algorithms):** These are like secret instructions that tell AI robots how to learn and solve problems. Think of them like recipes for baking a cake – they have steps to follow, but instead of flour and sugar, they use math and code!

3. **Robot Brain Power (GPUs & TPUs):** Just like our brains need energy to think, AI robots need special super-powerful computer chips to do their learning and thinking. These chips are called GPUs and TPUs, and

they're like rocket boosters for robot brains!

4. **Robot Teachers (Humans)**: Even though AI robots are super smart, they still need a little help from their human friends. Humans teach them what's right and wrong, help them learn from their mistakes, and make sure they use their powers for good.

5. **Robot Memory (Storage)**: To remember all the amazing things they learn, AI robots need a place to store their knowledge. It's like a giant library inside their digital brain!

6. **Robot Building Blocks** (Frameworks & Libraries): These are like pre-made parts for building AI robots. They make it easier for robot creators to put together all the pieces and make the robots work.

7. **Robot Language (Code)**: This is the special language that humans use to talk to robots and tell them what to do. It's like a secret code that only robots and their human friends understand!

Your AI Toolkit: Everything You Need to Unleash the Power of AI

Here's a breakdown of the key things needed to use AI, whether you're a researcher, developer, or simply interested in applying AI:

Hardware:

Hardware is the physical parts of a computer or machine that you can touch and see. Simple examples are keyboard, mouse, memory and processing chips inside the computers etc.

- **GPUs (Graphics Processing Units):** Originally designed for rendering graphics, GPUs have become the workhorse for AI, particularly for training deep learning models. They are specialized processors designed to handle large amounts of mathematical calculations simultaneously.

- **TPUs (Tensor Processing Units):** Designed specifically for AI workloads, TPUs are custom-designed chips optimized for tensor operations (the core building blocks of neural networks). They offer even greater speed and efficiency than GPUs for specific AI tasks.

- **CPUs (Central Processing Units):** While not as powerful as GPUs or TPUs for AI, CPUs are still essential for general tasks like managing data, running operating systems, and handling less computationally intensive AI operations.

- **Memory (RAM and Storage):** AI models often require vast amounts of data for training and inference (making predictions). Sufficient RAM is crucial for storing data during processing, while ample storage is needed to house large datasets and trained models.

Software:

Software is the invisible brain that tells the computer what to do and how to do it. Some examples are operating systems, your email software or calendar software etc.

- **Frameworks and Libraries:** These are pre-built tools and functionalities that make it easier to develop and deploy AI models. Popular examples include:

    - **TensorFlow:** An open-source machine learning framework developed by Google, providing a comprehensive ecosystem for building and deploying a wide range of machine learning models, from simple linear regression to complex neural networks. It offers flexibility and scalability, enabling users to run models on various hardware platforms, including CPUs, GPUs, and TPUs.
    - **PyTorch:** A powerful open-source deep learning framework known for its flexibility and dynamic computation graphs. It provides tools to build

and train neural networks using tensors (multidimensional arrays) and automatic differentiation for efficient gradient calculation.
- **Keras:** A user-friendly deep learning library built on top of TensorFlow, designed to simplify the creation and training of neural networks. It provides high-level building blocks and intuitive APIs, making it easier for both beginners and experts to experiment with and deploy deep learning models.

- **Algorithms:** These are the mathematical instructions that guide how AI models learn from data and make decisions. There are many different types of algorithms, each suited for different tasks, such as:

  - **Supervised Learning:** The model learns from labeled examples. (Don't worry, we will cover this later)
  - **Unsupervised Learning:** The model finds patterns in unlabeled data.
  - **Reinforcement Learning:** The model learns by interacting with an environment and receiving rewards or penalties. We will learn about this later.

- **Data Management Tools:** These help to clean, pre-process, and organize data, which is a critical step before training AI models. Popular tools include Pandas, Apache Spark etc.

Data:

Remember, this is the food that powers your AI systems!

- **Large, High-Quality Datasets:** The performance of an AI model is directly linked to the quality and quantity of data it's trained on. Large and diverse datasets that accurately represent the real world are essential for building robust and generalizable AI systems.

- **Data Annotation:** For supervised learning, data needs to be labeled with the correct answers, which can be a time-consuming and costly process. However, labeled data is essential for teaching AI models to make accurate predictions.

Expertise: Yes, all of us are the experts of AI. In some shape and form, we are providing the knowledge to the AI models to think like our brains.

- **AI Developers and Researchers:** People with skills in machine learning, data science, and software engineering are essential for developing, deploying, and maintaining AI systems. They need to understand the underlying algorithms, choose the right tools and frameworks, and address ethical considerations.

Other Important Considerations:

- **Cloud Computing:** Cloud platforms (like Google Cloud, AWS or Microsoft Azure) offer scalable computing resources for training and deploying AI models, making it more accessible to businesses and individuals without large IT infrastructure.

- **Edge Computing:** Sometimes, AI processing needs to happen on the device itself (like on a smartphone or a smart speaker) due to latency, privacy, or connectivity concerns.

- **Ethical and Responsible AI:** As AI becomes more powerful, it's crucial to ensure that it's developed and used responsibly, addressing issues like bias, fairness, transparency, and accountability.

So, next time you see a cool AI robot doing something

amazing, remember that it's all thanks to this awesome recipe of data, algorithms, brainpower, human teachers, memory, building blocks, and secret code!

Data: The Superfood for AI Brains!

When you teach a puppy new tricks, You'd show them what to do over and over again until they get it right. That's kind of how it works with AI, except instead of treats, AI uses data to learn and grow smarter.

Data is like the fuel for AI's brain. It can be anything: pictures of cute kittens, silly songs, lists of numbers, or even your chat messages with friends. The more data AI has, the better it understands the world and can do all sorts of cool stuff.

Think of it like this:

- **Pizza Pictures**: If an AI sees tons of pizza pictures, it can learn what pizza looks like and tell it apart from other foods.

- **Talking Time**. By listening to lots of conversations, AI learns how people talk and can understand what you say to it, like a smart friend!

- **Driving Data**: Self-driving cars get super smart by looking at millions of miles of road data. They learn to recognize traffic signs, other cars, and even pedestrians.

- **Music Mania**: AI that listens to lots of songs learns about different styles and instruments. It can then create its own catchy tunes!

When you encounter an AI tool next time, remember that it got super smart by munching on lots and lots of data! It's like a never-ending buffet for AI brains!

Algorithms: AI's Secret Instruction Manual!

Let's say, you're building a spaceship from toy blocks. You have all the pieces, but you need instructions to put them together correctly. Those **instructions are like algorithms for AI**!

Algorithms are a set of step-by-step rules that tell AI exactly what to do. They are like a recipe for AI, guiding it on how to solve problems and make decisions.

Different algorithms are used for different tasks:

- **Learning Algorithms:** These algorithms help AI learn from data, like figuring out what a cat looks like by seeing lots of cat pictures.

- **Decision-Making Algorithms:** These help AI make choices, like which song to recommend you based on your favorite music.

- **Driving Algorithms:** These help self-driving cars figure out how to stay safe on the road, like knowing when to stop at a red light or go around an obstacle.

- **Art Algorithms:** These help AI create amazing paintings or compose music, like giving it a magical paintbrush or musical instrument.

Just like a good recipe can make a delicious dish, a good algorithm can make AI super smart and capable!

Think of algorithms like a secret code that unlocks AI's superpowers! By creating and improving these instructions, we can teach AI to do amazing things that help us and make our world even more awesome.

Machine Learning: AI's Superpowered Training!

When you train a puppy to fetch, You start with simple steps, rewarding them for progress, and eventually, they master the trick! Machine learning is like that for AI – it's the secret training method that helps AI get super smart!

Instead of treats and belly rubs, AI learns from data. Think of it like this:

- **Picture Puzzles:** You show AI tons of pictures of cats and dogs, and it learns to tell them apart by finding patterns.

- **Song Matchmaker:** By listening to your favorite tunes, AI learns your music taste and suggests new songs you might like.

- **Word Wizard:** AI reads millions of books and articles to learn how to write stories, answer questions, or even translate languages.

But it's not just about memorizing facts. AI uses clever algorithms (special instructions) to find hidden patterns and relationships in all that data. It's like putting together a giant jigsaw puzzle to reveal a complete picture.

Once AI has learned enough, it can use that knowledge to do amazing things, like:

- Recognizing objects in photos or videos

- Understanding human language

- Diagnosing diseases from medical scans

- Driving cars safely

- Creating art and music that rivals human creations!

The coolest part? The more AI learns, the better it gets at its tasks, just like you do when you practice a new skill. It's like AI is leveling up its abilities every day!

TPUs & Tensors: Powering AI's Super Brain!

If your brain had a special chip that helped you do math problems super fast! That's kind of what a TPU (Tensor Processing Unit) is for AI. It's a special chip designed by Google, specifically to help AI think faster and learn more efficiently.

What are TPUs?

- **Super Speedy Calculations**: TPUs are like turbo-charged calculators, designed to do the specific types of math that AI models need to learn and make decisions. They can crunch through numbers way faster than regular computer chips, which means AI can learn and improve at lightning speed!

- **Made for Tensors**: TPUs are specially built to handle tensors, which are the building blocks of many AI models. Think of tensors like multi-dimensional arrays of numbers. They can represent all sorts of information, like the colors in an image, the words in a sentence, or the moves in a chess game. TPUs are experts at handling these tensors, making them the perfect tools for powering AI's super brain.

- **Cloud Power**: You don't need a special computer to use TPUs! They're usually found in massive data centers called "the cloud," where they work together with other TPUs to train and run complex AI models. It's like a giant playground for AI, where they can learn and play together!

What are Tensors?

- **Building Blocks of Data**: Tensors are like the building blocks of AI. They're the fundamental building blocks that AI models use to represent and process information.

- **Multi-Dimensional Arrays:** Tensors can be thought of as multi-dimensional arrays of numbers. Imagine a single number is like a dot, a list of numbers is like a line, a table of numbers is like a square, and a cube of numbers is like a 3D shape. Tensors can have even more dimensions, making them super flexible for representing complex data like images, sounds, and text.

- **The Language of AI:** Tensors are the language that AI models use to communicate with each other. They represent the input data that the model receives, the calculations it performs, and the output it produces. By understanding tensors, you can peek inside the AI's brain and see how it thinks!

Why do we need TPUs?

AI models are getting bigger and more complex, which means they need more computing power to learn and make decisions. TPUs are specifically designed to accelerate these AI tasks, making them faster, more efficient, and more powerful. This is crucial for developing new AI technologies that can solve real-world problems like climate change, disease prediction, and language translation.

So, the next time you see an AI model doing something amazing, remember that it's all thanks to the power of TPUs and tensors! They're the unsung heroes that are powering the AI revolution and making our world a smarter place.

Unveiling the Layers of Intelligence: AI, Machine Learning, and Deep Learning

Artificial Intelligence (AI), Machine Learning (ML), and Deep Learning (DL) are often used interchangeably, but they represent distinct concepts with a hierarchical relationship. Let's delve into their key differences:

1. Artificial Intelligence (AI):

- **Broadest Scope**: AI is the umbrella term encompassing any technique that enables machines to mimic human intelligence. This can range from simple rule-based systems to complex algorithms that can learn and adapt.

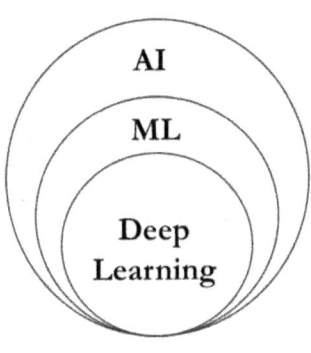

- **Goals**: The ultimate goal of AI is to create systems that can reason, problem-solve, understand language, perceive the environment, and even exhibit creativity.

- **Examples**: AI applications are diverse, including virtual assistants like Google home and Siri, recommendation systems on platforms like Netflix, and autonomous vehicles.

2. Machine Learning (ML):

- **Subset of AI**: ML is a specific approach within AI that focuses on algorithms that can learn from data without being explicitly programmed. These algorithms build models based on patterns in data, which can then be used to make predictions or decisions.

- **Types**: There are various types of ML algorithms, including supervised learning (where the model is trained on labeled data), unsupervised learning (where the model identifies patterns in unlabeled data), and reinforcement learning (where the model learns through trial and error).

- **Examples**: ML is used in spam filters, fraud detection systems, image recognition software, and language translation tools.

3. Deep Learning (DL):

- **Subset of ML**: DL is a specialized subfield of ML that utilizes artificial neural networks (ANNs) with multiple layers to process and learn from complex data. These neural networks are inspired by the structure and function of the human brain.

- Complex Data Handling: DL excels at handling unstructured data like images, audio, and text, making it ideal for tasks such as image classification, speech recognition, and natural language processing.

- **Examples**: DL powers advanced technologies like facial recognition in smartphones, medical image analysis for disease detection, and the sophisticated language generation capabilities of models like GPT-3.

In Summary:

- AI is the overarching field, seeking to create intelligent machines.

- ML is a subset of AI that enables machines to learn from data.

- DL is a specialized type of ML that uses neural networks to tackle complex tasks.

Understanding these distinctions is crucial for navigating the rapidly evolving landscape of artificial intelligence and its potential impact on various industries and aspects of our lives.

Understanding Encoding and Decoding

Computers, like robots, don't speak our language. They only understand numbers (and lots of them!). Encoding and decoding are the translators that bridge this gap. If you have a secret message you want to send to a friend, below are the steps in the language of encoding and decoding.

- **Encoding**: You translate the message into a code that only you and your friend understand. This could be a special language, symbols, or a different way of writing the letters.

- **Decoding**: Your friend receives the coded message and translates it back into the original language so they can read it.

This is similar to what computers do with information:

- **Encoding**: The computer takes information, like a

picture or a document, and translates it into a code it can understand. This code is usually made up of numbers.

- **Decoding**: The computer takes the code and translates it back into the original information so we can see the picture or read the document.

This process allows AI to do amazing things like:

- **Understand your questions** and respond in a meaningful way.

- **Translate languages** by encoding words in one language and decoding them into another.

- **Create images** from text descriptions by encoding the words and then decoding the result as pixels.

- **Recognize faces** by encoding an image and comparing it to a database of encoded faces.

Without encoding and decoding, AI wouldn't be able to understand or interact with the world in a way that's useful to us.

AI Building Blocks Challenge:

1. Data Detective

Mission: Collect data about your favorite things!
What to do: Write down your favorite foods and animals.

Food

_____

_____

Animals

_____

_____

Find pictures or videos of these things online. Make a list of the words you use most often when talking about them.

Food

_____

_____

Animal

_____

_____

Do you see a pattern yet?

💡 **Why it matters:** This helps you understand how AI collects and uses data to learn

2. Algorithm Architect:

Mission: Design a simple algorithm (set of instructions) to help a robot make a sandwich.

What to do: Write down each step involved in making a sandwich, from getting the bread to adding the toppings. Be specific and detailed, so the robot knows exactly what to do!

_____
_____
_____
_____
_____
_____
_____

💡 **Why it matters:** This helps you understand how AI uses algorithms to follow instructions and complete tasks.

3. Model Mastermind:

Mission: You're an AI model learning to recognize different types of animals.

What to do: Look at pictures of different animals (cats, dogs, birds, etc.). Identify the features that make each animal unique, like fur, feathers, or wings.

_____
_____
_____
_____
_____
_____

Practice classifying new animal pictures based on these features.

_____
_____
_____
_____
_____
_____
_____

💡 Why it matters: This helps you understand how AI models learn from examples and use patterns to make predictions.

The Science Behind AI: A Fun and Easy Explanation

Now we are all thinking of AI as a super-smart robot friend who can learn and do things on its own, just like a human! But how does this happen? Well, it's all thanks to some cool scientific concepts that have been around for a while, but have recently gotten even more powerful:

1. Machine Learning (ML): Learning from Experience

- **The History:** In the 1950s, scientists started to wonder if computers could learn like humans. They created algorithms (step-by-step instructions) that allowed computers to improve their performance on tasks by analyzing data.

- **How It Works:** If you're teaching a robot to recognize cats, You show it thousands of pictures of cats, and it learns the common features: pointy ears, whiskers, furry bodies. Now, when you show it a new picture, it can guess if it's a cat or not!

- **Current State:** Today, ML is used everywhere! It's how your phone suggests words, how your video streaming service recommends movies, and even how doctors diagnose diseases by AI analyzing digital images of scans.

2. Neural Networks: The Brainpower Behind AI

- **The History:** In the 1940s, scientists started to study how the human brain works. They noticed it's made of billions of tiny cells called neurons that communicate with each other. They then tried to create artificial neurons in computers.

- **How It Works:** Artificial neural networks (ANNs) are like a simplified version of the brain. They have layers of interconnected nodes (like neurons) that process information. The more data they process, the better they get at recognizing patterns and making decisions.

- **Current State:** ANNs are the secret sauce behind many modern AI systems. They power language translation, image recognition, and even self-driving cars!

3. Deep Learning: Supercharging AI

- **The History:** In the 2010s, scientists found a way to make ANNs much more powerful by adding many more layers of nodes. They called it deep learning.

- **How It Works:** Deep learning allows AI to tackle

more complex tasks, like understanding natural language and generating creative content. Deep learning is like teaching a computer to recognize things by showing it lots of examples. It has many layers of connections inside, like a brain, that it uses to figure out patterns and details. With each example it sees, the computer strengthens the connections that lead to the right answer and weakens the ones that don't. This way, it learns to recognize things it hasn't seen before based on the patterns it has learned.

- **Current State:** Deep learning is driving the latest breakthroughs in AI. It's how AI chatbots can have conversations, how AI can create realistic images, and how scientists are even using AI to design new drugs.

4. Natural Language Processing (NLP): Teaching AI to Talk

- **The History:** For decades, scientists have been trying to get computers to understand and use human language. Early attempts were simple and rule-based, but they weren't very good at handling the nuances of human communication.

- **How It Works:** NLP uses ML and deep learning to teach AI to understand, generate, and translate human language. It analyzes vast amounts of text data to learn grammar, syntax, and even the different meanings of words in context.

- **Current State:** NLP is what powers chatbots, language translators, and voice assistants like Siri and Alexa. It's getting so good that it's hard to tell if you're talking to a human or a machine sometimes!

It's an Exciting Time for AI!

The science behind AI is evolving rapidly. With new discoveries and advancements happening all the time, we're just scratching the surface of what AI can do. So stay tuned, because the future of AI is going to be amazing!

Let us dive deeper into some of these important concepts that powers our future

What is Machine Learning

Imagine teaching a computer to be smart, without explicitly telling it the rules. That's what machine learning (ML) is all about! It's like giving a computer the ability to learn from experience and make predictions or decisions based on patterns it finds in data.

Here's how it works:

1. **Gather data:** First, we feed the computer tons of data.

It could be anything, like pictures of cats and dogs, sales figures, weather reports, or even the words you use in your emails.

2. **Train the model:** Next, the computer uses clever algorithms (special instructions) to find patterns and relationships in the data. It builds a model, which is like a set of rules that can help it make sense of new information.

3. **Make predictions:** Once the model is trained, we can give it new data and ask it to make predictions. For example, we can show it a new picture and ask if it's a cat or dog, or analyze a customer's past purchases to recommend products they might like.

The Different Ways AI Learns: It's Like School for Robots!

Just like you learn in different ways at school, AI has different ways to learn too! These different learning styles are called "**types of machine learning.**" Let's explore them together:

1. **Supervised Learning: Learning with a Teacher**

   Do you remember, When your teacher showed you

pictures of apples and oranges and told you which picture is which fruit? That's how supervised learning works! AI gets a bunch of examples with the right answers (like labeled pictures of fruit), and it learns to recognize patterns so it can tell the difference between apples and oranges in new pictures.

This type of learning is used for tasks like:

- Recognizing objects in pictures (like identifying cats or dogs)
- Filtering spam emails
- Understanding and translating languages

2. **Unsupervised Learning: Exploring on Your Own**

Unsupervised learning is like, you're given a box of different colored blocks, and you have to sort them into groups without any instructions. That's what unsupervised learning is like for AI! It gets data without any labels and tries to find patterns and similarities all by itself.

This type of learning is used for tasks like:

- Recommending products you might like based on your past purchases

- Finding hidden patterns in data to detect fraud

- Grouping customers with similar interests for marketing campaigns

3. **Reinforcement Learning: Learning from Experience**

Imagine playing a video game where you get points for doing good things and lose points for making mistakes. You learn how to play better by trying different things and seeing what works. That's how reinforcement learning works for AI! It learns by trying different actions and getting feedback (rewards or punishments) based on how well it does.

This type of learning is used for tasks like:

- Playing games like chess or Go

- Training robots to walk or grasp objects

- Teaching self-driving cars to navigate roads safely

These are the main types of machine learning, but AI is

constantly evolving, and there are always new and exciting ways for it to learn! By understanding how AI learns, we can better appreciate the amazing things it can do and how it's changing our world.

⚠ Jargon alert ⚠

What is a Model - When you are teaching a pet new tricks, You show them examples and reward them when they get it right.

Machine learning models are similar!

They learn by looking at examples (data) and finding **patterns**. These models get smarter over time as they see more examples, just like a dog who becomes an expert at fetching with practice!

In the end, these models can use what they've learned to make predictions or decisions, like telling you if a picture is of a cat or a dog.

What is a Pattern - Imagine teaching a robot to sort toys. You show it many examples of cars, dolls, and blocks, and it learns to recognize the shapes, colors, and sizes that make each toy different. These shapes, colors, and sizes are like patterns.

In machine learning, a pattern is something that repeats or occurs regularly in data. It's like a hidden code that the model learns to crack, allowing it to make predictions or decisions. For example, a model that's seen many pictures of cats will learn the patterns that make up a cat's face and body, so  it can recognize new pictures of cats it hasn't seen before.

Just like your robot friend can now sort toys easily, a machine learning model can use the patterns it learns to solve all sorts of problems!

Here are some real-life examples of machine learning in action:

- **Email spam filters:** ML analyzes your emails and learns to identify spam messages, keeping your inbox clean.

- **Product recommendations:** Online stores use ML to suggest products you might be interested in based on your past purchases or browsing history.

- **Voice assistants:** Siri, Alexa, and Google Assistant use ML to understand your voice commands and answer your questions.

- **Fraud detection:** Banks use ML to analyze transactions and detect suspicious activity that could be fraud.

- **Image recognition:** ML can be used to identify objects, people, or even emotions in pictures and videos. This is how Facebook automatically tags your friends in photos.

- **Medical diagnosis:** ML can help doctors analyze medical images (like X-rays and MRIs) to diagnose diseases more accurately.

- **Self-driving cars:** ML helps self-driving cars understand their surroundings and make decisions about how to navigate safely.

These are just a few of the many ways machine learning is used in our everyday lives. It's a powerful tool that can help us solve problems, make better decisions, and even create new products and services.

What are neural networks

Neural networks are the heart of many Artificial Intelligence (AI) systems. Inspired by the human brain, they enable computers to learn and make decisions like we do.

How they work:

Our brain is a network of interconnected neurons. In AI's neural network, these neurons are replaced by mathematical functions, which work together to process information. Each connection has a weight, representing its importance. The network receives input (data like images, text, or numbers), processes it through the layers of interconnected neurons, and produces output (a decision, prediction, or classification).

As the network is trained on data, it adjusts the weights of these connections, learning patterns and improving its performance over time. This learning process is similar to how our brain strengthens certain connections as we gain experience.

Examples of Neural Networks in Action:

1. **Image Recognition:** Neural networks can be trained to identify objects in images, such as cats, dogs, or even traffic signs. This is how your phone's photo app automatically organizes pictures or how self-driving cars can "see" the road.

2. **Natural Language Processing (NLP):** Neural networks are crucial for NLP tasks, like language translation, sentiment analysis, and chatbot interactions. This is how Google Translate can convert text from one language to another or how your email filters out spam.

3. **Recommender Systems:** Have you ever noticed how Netflix or Amazon recommends movies or products you might like? That's often powered by neural networks, which analyze your past behavior to predict what you'll enjoy next.

4. **Fraud Detection:** Banks and financial institutions use neural networks to detect fraudulent transactions by identifying unusual patterns in data.

5. **Medical Diagnosis:** Neural networks can analyze medical images like X-rays and MRIs to help doctors detect diseases like cancer earlier and more accurately.

6. **Weather Forecasting:** Neural networks can analyze vast amounts of weather data to make more precise predictions about temperature, precipitation, and other conditions.

7. **Game Playing:** Neural networks have famously defeated human champions in games like chess and Go, showcasing their ability to learn strategies and outsmart opponents.

What is Natural Language Processing? Natural Language Processing (NLP) is like teaching computers to be language experts! It's a type of AI that focuses on helping computers understand, interpret, and generate human language. This technology works by using special algorithms to analyze text and speech, looking for patterns and meaning.  With NLP, computers can translate languages, power chatbots, analyze the sentiment of text, summarize long documents, and even filter out spam emails. NLP is constantly improving, becoming better at understanding the nuances and complexities of human language, leading to even more impressive applications in the future. We can anticipate super-smart virtual assistants, AI-powered writing tools, and enhanced communication between people from different cultures. NLP is transforming how we interact with technology, making it more intuitive and accessible for everyone.

Superpowered Smarts Challenge: Decoding the Secrets of AI!

Ready to unlock the mysteries of AI's superpowered brain? Let's dive into the key characteristics that make AI so amazing and test your knowledge with these fun exercises:

1. Pattern Recognition Power-Up:

Mission: Become a pattern detective and train your own AI!

What to do: Gather a collection of objects, like toys, clothes, or even food items. Sort them into groups based on different patterns (color, shape, size, etc.). Try to explain the rules you used to create the groups.

_____
_____
_____
_____
_____
_____
_____
_____
_____

Imagine you're teaching an AI model to do the same task. How would you explain the patterns to it?

💡 Why it matters: This helps you understand how AI uses pattern recognition to identify objects, classify data, and make predictions.

2. The Language of Learning Challenge:

Mission: Learn the secret language of AI!

What to do: Create a list of 10 words or phrases related to AI (e.g., algorithm, machine learning, neural network). Look up the definitions of each word and write them in your own words. Challenge a friend or family member to an AI vocabulary quiz!

💡 Why it matters: This helps you understand the terminology of AI and communicate effectively with others about this exciting technology.

3. Creative AI Storyteller:

Mission: Unleash your imagination and write a short story about AI!

What to do: Imagine a world where AI has advanced even further. What can it do? How does it interact with humans? Create characters who are AI robots or humans who work with AI. Write a story that explores the possibilities and challenges of living in a world with intelligent machines.

💡 Why it matters: This exercise encourages you to think creatively about the future of AI and its potential impact on our lives.

AI is Everywhere! Even in Your Pocket!

Superpowered Smartphones: AI in Your Pocket!

Your smartphone is like a tiny computer, but did you know it has a secret weapon that makes it extra awesome? Artificial Intelligence (AI)! It's like having a mini superhero right in your pocket, ready to help you with all sorts of things.

🔋 From Simple to Super:

Just a few years ago, smartphones were mostly used for calls and texts. But thanks to AI, they've become super-smart! In fact, the average smartphone today is more powerful than the computers that were used to send astronauts to the moon!

- **Processing Power:** In just five years, the average smartphone's processing speed has increased by over 60%. That means your phone can now do things that were impossible just a few years ago, like recognizing faces or translating languages in real time.

- **Storage Capacity:** Remember those old phones with tiny memories? Not anymore! Today, many smartphones have enough storage to hold thousands of photos, videos, and apps. In fact, the average storage capacity has increased by over 100% in the last five years.

- **Camera Quality:** Smartphone cameras have gotten so good, they can rival professional cameras! With AI-powered features like portrait mode and night mode, you can take stunning photos even in challenging conditions.

AI on the Edge: Superpowers in Your Palm!

One of the coolest things about AI in smartphones is something called "edge computing." This means that instead of sending all your data to a giant computer somewhere else, a lot of the AI processing happens right on your phone. This makes things faster, more private, and even saves your battery life!

Here are some ways AI is already making your phone super, thanks to edge computing:

- **Super Snaps:** Your phone can automatically recognize faces, blur backgrounds, and even suggest the best filters for your photos, all without sending your pictures to the cloud.

- **Voice Wizardry:** Voice assistants like Siri and Google Assistant use on-device AI to understand your commands and respond instantly.

- **Smart Typing:** AI-powered keyboards learn your typing style and predict your next word, making typing faster and easier.

- **Real-Time Translation:** Some apps can translate text or speech in real time, right on your phone, so you can chat with someone who speaks a different language without any delays.

- **Personalized Recommendations:** Your phone can analyze your app usage and suggest new apps you might like, or even customize your home screen with widgets you'll find most useful.

The Future is in Your Pocket!

With AI getting smarter every day, your smartphone will only become even more amazing! Imagine having a virtual assistant that can understand your emotions, a language translator that whispers in your ear, or a personal health coach that tracks your well-being. All of these possibilities (and more!) are just waiting to be unlocked, thanks to the power of AI in your pocket.

AI Knows Your Secrets! (Well, Some of Them)

How does AI know what you want before you even ask? It's like having a mind-reading best friend! Well, not exactly, but it does use some clever tricks to understand your preferences and interests.

Data Detective: AI can collect information about you from all sorts of places (If you have given the permission to do so)

- **Websites You Visit:** AI can track what you click on, how long you stay on a page, and what you put in your shopping cart.

- **Social Media Sleuth:** It looks at the posts you like, the comments you make, and the people you follow.

- **Your Voice Commands:** If you use voice assistants like Siri or Alexa, if they're listening (Active listening) to what you say and learning about your interests. Depending on the permissions granted

- **Your Purchases:** Online stores keep track of what you buy and can even predict what you might want to buy next.

Thinking Cap Time: Once AI collects all this data, it uses its super-smart algorithms to analyze it. It looks for patterns in your behavior, like:

- What kinds of videos do you like to watch?

- What topics are you interested in?

- What products are you likely to buy?

Making Your Life Easier: AI uses all this information to make your life better in all sorts of ways:

- **Personalized Recommendations:** Netflix knows what movies you might like, Spotify suggests new songs, and Amazon shows you products you might be interested in buying.

- **Smart Assistants:** Siri and Alexa can answer your questions, set reminders, and even control your smart home devices.

- **Better Search Results:** Google uses AI to understand what you're searching for and provide you with the most relevant results.

Protecting Your Privacy: It's important to be careful about what information you share online. Here are some tips for staying safe:

- **Read Privacy Policies:** Before you use a website or

app, read its privacy policy to understand what data they collect and how they use it.

- **Adjust Your Settings:** Most apps and websites have privacy settings that let you control what information is shared.

- **Use Strong Passwords:** Protect your accounts with strong passwords and change them regularly.

- **Be Aware of What You Share:** Think twice before sharing personal information online, especially on public forums or social media.

Remember, AI is a powerful tool, but it's important to use it responsibly. By being mindful of your privacy and using AI wisely, you can enjoy all the benefits it offers without compromising your personal information.

Talking Tech: Chatting with Your AI Sidekick!

Ever wondered how your voice commands magically turn into actions when you talk to your AI assistant? It's like having a conversation with a super-smart friend! Let's dive into the science behind this chatty technology and see how it's making life easier and more fun.

From Soundwaves to Super-Smart Answers: The Journey of a Voice Command

1. **Capturing Your Voice:** When you say, "Hey Google, what's the weather like today?" your smartphone's microphone picks up the vibrations of your voice, just like a tiny drum.

2. **Converting to Code:** The microphone sends these vibrations to your phone's brain, a tiny but powerful computer chip. This chip converts the soundwaves into a special code that computers can understand, called digital signals.

3. **Sending to the Cloud:** These digital signals are sent super-fast through the internet to a giant team of computers in the cloud. These computers are like a hive of super-smart bees, working together to understand your command.

4. **Natural Language Processing (NLP) Magic:** The computers in the cloud use a special type of AI called Natural Language Processing (NLP) to figure out what you said. It's like a super-powered language detective, decoding your words and figuring out what you mean.

5. **Finding the Answer:** Once the AI understands your question, it searches through a massive library of information (like a giant encyclopedia!) to find the answer. This could be information about the weather, the latest news, or even the score of your favorite sports

team.

6. **Text-to-Speech Transformation:** The answer is then converted from text back into speech using another type of AI called Text-to-Speech (TTS). It's like a voice actor reading the answer out loud.

7. **Back to Your Ears:** The AI assistant sends the spoken answer back to your phone, which plays it through the speaker so you can hear the answer to your question.

This whole process happens in the blink of an eye, making it feel like you're having a real-time conversation with your AI assistant.

Real-Life Examples of Chatty AI

- Google Assistant and Siri on your smartphone: They can answer questions, set alarms, send messages, and even play your favorite music.

- Google Home and other smart speakers: They control your smart home devices, tell you the news, and even read you bedtime stories.

- Chatbots on websites and apps: They can help you find information, troubleshoot problems, or even just have a friendly chat.

The Future of Chatty AI

In the future, AI assistants will become even more intelligent and capable:

- They'll understand your emotions and intentions, making conversations more natural and empathetic.

- They'll be able to learn more about your interests and preferences, offering personalized recommendations and suggestions.

- They'll become experts in various fields, providing specialized help and advice on topics like health, finance, and education.

AI assistants will be like our trusted sidekicks, helping us with everyday tasks, answering our questions, and even keeping us company when we're feeling lonely. They'll be there for us whenever we need them, making our lives easier and more enjoyable. So, get ready to chat with AI assistants – the future is full of possibilities!

Discover the Hidden Superpowers of Your Smartphone!

Your smartphone is way more than just a device for calls and games. It's packed with AI superpowers, making it your own personal genie! Let's put on our detective hats and uncover the AI magic hidden inside your pocket:

1. AI App Investigator

Mission: Explore your phone for apps that use AI.

What to do:

- Open your favorite apps and look for features that seem smart or personalized. Do you see recommendations for videos, music, or products? Does your phone automatically categorize your photos or offer smart replies in your messaging app? These are all clues that AI is at work!

- Make a list of the apps you find that use AI. Try to guess how AI is helping you in each app.

- Share your findings with your friends or family and see if they can spot any other AI-powered features on their phones.

💡 Why it matters: This helps you understand how AI is already integrated into your daily life and the many ways it enhances your digital experiences.

2. Voice Assistant Interviewer

Mission: Chat with your voice assistant and learn how AI understands you.

What to do:

- Activate your phone's voice assistant (Google Assistant or Siri or Bixby or any other).

- Ask it questions about the weather, your schedule, or even random trivia.

- Notice how it responds to your voice and how it understands what you're saying.

- Try asking it to do something for you, like setting a timer or playing a song.

- Share your most interesting or funny conversations with your voice assistant with others.

💡 Why it matters: This helps you understand how AI uses natural language processing (NLP) to understand your voice commands and respond in a helpful way.

3. Treasure Hunt for AI Features

Mission: Dig deeper into your phone's settings and explore hidden AI features.

What to do:

- Go to your phone's settings and look for options related to AI or machine learning.

- See if you can find features like adaptive battery usage, smart suggestions for apps, or even AI-based security features.

- Experiment with these features and see how they can make your phone more personalized and efficient.

💡 Why it matters: This helps you uncover the hidden AI capabilities of your phone and learn how AI is constantly working behind the scenes to improve your user experience.

Generative AI: The Imagination Machine!

Generative AI is like having a magic wand that could create anything you can dream of, from fantastical creatures to beautiful paintings! Well, that's kind of what Generative AI is like! It's a type of Artificial Intelligence that can create new things all by itself, just like a super-creative artist or inventor.

What Can Generative AI Do?

- **Paintings and Drawings:** Generative AI can create beautiful and unique artwork in various styles, just by giving it a few words or a simple sketch. It's like having a personal artist who's always ready to paint your dreams!
- **Music and Sound Effects:** It can compose original music, from catchy pop tunes to dramatic orchestral pieces. It can even create realistic sound effects for games and movies. It's like having your own band or sound studio right in your computer!
- **Stories and Poems:** Generative AI can write creative

stories, poems, and even scripts for plays and movies. It can come up with new characters, plot twists, and dialogue that will surprise and delight you. It's like having a professional writer to help you unleash your imagination!
- **Realistic Photos and Videos:** Generative AI can create images and videos that are so realistic, it's hard to tell them apart from real ones. This technology is being used to create special effects in movies, realistic avatars for video games, and even virtual models for fashion shows. It's like having a movie director and special effects team at your disposal!
- **Designs and Patterns:** Generative AI can generate unique designs for clothes, furniture, buildings, and even jewelry. It can also create interesting patterns for textiles, wallpaper, and other materials. It's like having a fashion designer, architect, and interior decorator all in one!

What Should You Learn About Generative AI?

- **How it Works:** Generative AI uses complex algorithms and neural networks to learn patterns from existing data. It then uses this knowledge to create new and original content that has never existed before.
- **What it Can Do:** As we saw above, Generative AI has a wide range of applications in art, music, writing, design, and even science and technology. It's important to understand its capabilities and limitations to make the most of it.

- **How to Use it:** There are many tools and platforms available that allow you to experiment with Generative AI. Try generating images from text descriptions, creating your own music, or even writing a story with the help of AI.
- **Ethical Considerations:** It's important to think about the ethical implications of Generative AI. For example, how can we ensure that it's used for good and not for creating fake or harmful content? How do we protect artists and creators from having their work copied or misused by AI?

The Future of Generative AI

Generative AI is a rapidly evolving field with incredible potential. As it becomes more sophisticated, we can expect it to revolutionize the way we create and experience art, music, design, and other forms of creative expression. Who knows, maybe one day you'll even be able to create your own AI-powered masterpiece!

Remember, the possibilities are endless! With creativity and curiosity, you can explore the amazing world of Generative AI and discover new ways to express yourself and make a positive impact on the world.

Unleashing Your Inner Artist with Generative AI: Top Tools and Tips!

Ready to unleash your creativity with the help of AI? Here are some of the most popular and accessible tools you can use to explore the amazing world of generative AI, including models from tech giants like Google and Meta:

1. **Image Generation:**

- **DALL-E 2 (OpenAI):** Famous for generating stunning images from text descriptions, DALL-E 2 is like having a personal illustrator who can bring your wildest ideas to life.
  - **Model:** DALL-E 2 uses a powerful transformer-based language model to understand your text and a diffusion model to generate the corresponding image.
  - **Tip:** Be specific and descriptive in your text prompt, including details like style, colors, and mood.
- **Imagen (Google):** Google's Imagen is another text-to-image model known for its photorealistic and creative outputs.

- **Model:** Imagen also leverages a transformer-based language model for text understanding and a diffusion model for image creation.
- **Tip:** Experiment with different prompts and styles, as Imagen is capable of diverse artistic expressions.
- **Make-A-Scene (Meta):** This tool allows you to sketch out your vision and then have the AI fill in the details with stunning imagery.
  - **Model:** Make-A-Scene combines a language model with a generative adversarial network (GAN) to create images based on both your text and sketch input.
  - **Tip:** Don't worry if your sketches are rough; the AI can interpret your basic shapes and turn them into impressive visuals.
- **Midjourney:** This AI art generator is known for its beautiful, dreamlike images and has become a favorite among artists and designers. You can create images by typing commands in a chat-like interface.
  - **Model:** Midjourney uses a proprietary model based on diffusion techniques, similar to DALL-E 2.
  - **Tip:** Experiment with different prompts and styles to find your unique artistic voice and Explore Midjourney's community and forums for inspiration and to see what others are creating.
- **Stable Diffusion:** This open-source model has made image generation even more accessible, allowing users

to run it on their own computers or through online platforms. It's known for its versatility and the ability to create photorealistic images.

- **Model:** Stable Diffusion also uses a diffusion model for image generation.
- **Tip:** If you're tech-savvy, you can fine-tune Stable Diffusion with your own images to create personalized models that reflect your artistic style.

2. **Text Generation:**

- **ChatGPT (OpenAI):** This conversational AI model can answer questions, write stories, and even generate code snippets. Its versatility makes it a valuable tool for both creative and practical applications.
  - **Model:** ChatGPT is powered by the GPT family of large language models, trained on massive text datasets.
  - **Tip:** Provide clear instructions and context to get the most accurate and helpful responses.
- **LaMDA (Google):** This experimental conversational AI model is designed to engage in natural and open-ended dialogues on a wide range of topics.
  - **Model:** LaMDA is also a large language model, trained on diverse conversational data.

- **Tip:** Engage in free-flowing conversations with LaMDA to explore its potential for creative and informative interactions.
- **NovelAI:** This platform specializes in generating stories and creative text, making it a great resource for writers and storytellers seeking inspiration.
  - **Model:** NovelAI uses a customized version of the GPT model trained on a large dataset of creative writing.
  - **Tip:** Collaborate with the AI by providing initial ideas or prompts, and see where your creative journey takes you.

3. **Music Generation:**

- **MusicLM (Google):** This model can generate high-fidelity music from text descriptions, even matching the desired genre and instrumentation.
  - **Model:** MusicLM leverages a hierarchical sequence-to-sequence model trained on a large dataset of labeled music.
  - **Tip:** Be specific in your text descriptions, mentioning the genre, mood, instruments, and any other details that help define the music you want to hear.

- **Amper Music:** This tool allows you to create custom music tracks for videos, games, or any other project.
  - **Model:** Amper Music combines rule-based systems and machine learning to generate music.
  - **Tip:** Experiment with different combinations of instruments and styles to find the perfect sound for your project.
- **Jukebox:** Developed by OpenAI, Jukebox can generate music in different genres, from country to pop to classical. You can even ask it to create songs in the style of your favorite artists!
  - **Model:** Jukebox uses a complex neural network that has been trained on a massive dataset of songs.
  - **Tip:** Provide as much detail as possible about the genre, mood, and instrumentation you want to hear.

Remember, these are just a few examples of the many exciting tools and models available for generative AI. As you explore, remember:

- **Experimentation is Key:** Don't be afraid to try different prompts, styles, and combinations. The joy of generative AI is in discovering the unexpected and surprising results it can produce.
- **Collaboration is Cool:** Work with the AI as your creative partner. It can spark new ideas and help you overcome creative blocks.

Imagination Ignition: Unleash Your Creativity with Generative AI Exercises!

Get ready to flex your creative muscles and explore the amazing world of generative AI with these fun and interactive exercises:

1. **Text-to-Image Wizardry:**

Mission: Describe a scene, object, or character in vivid detail and let an AI model bring it to life as an image.

What to do:

- Choose a text-to-image AI model like DALL-E 2, Imagen, or Stable Diffusion.
- Think of a creative prompt, like "a fluffy cat wearing a pirate hat sailing on a ship made of cheese" or "a robot exploring a hidden jungle temple."
- Input your prompt into the AI model and see what amazing artwork it creates!
- Experiment with different prompts and styles to discover the endless possibilities of text-to-image generation.

💡 Why it matters: This exercise sparks your imagination and helps you understand how AI can transform words into visual art.

2. **Storytelling with AI:**

Mission: Collaborate with an AI model to write a unique and imaginative story.

What to do:

- Use a text generation tool like ChatGPT or NovelAI.
- Start with a simple prompt, like "a young adventurer discovers a hidden treasure map" or "a scientist invents a time machine."
- Let the AI model generate the next part of the story.
- Continue collaborating with the AI, adding your own twists and turns to the plot.
- See what amazing stories you can create together!

💡 Why it matters: This exercise encourages teamwork between humans and AI, showcasing the potential for creative collaboration and storytelling.

Large Language Models: The Word Wizards of AI

Have you ever chatted with a chatbot that seemed almost human? Or used a tool that magically wrote an essay for you? If so, you've probably encountered a Large Language Model (LLM)! They're the wordsmiths of the AI world, capable of understanding and generating text that is remarkably human-like. But how do they do it? Let's dive into the fascinating world of LLMs and their even more impressive cousins, multi-modal models!

What are Large Language Models?

Large Language Models or LLMs are a type of artificial intelligence that are trained on massive amounts of text data. This data can include books, articles, websites, code, and even social media conversations. By analyzing all this text, LLMs learn the patterns and structures of language, including grammar, vocabulary, and even the nuances of meaning and context.

Think of it like this: LLMs are like super-readers who have devoured an entire library! They have absorbed so much knowledge about language that they can now understand and generate text on a wide range of topics.

How Do LLMs Work?

At their core, LLMs are powered by neural networks, a type of AI model inspired by the human brain. These networks consist of layers of interconnected nodes (like neurons) that process information. When an LLM receives a text input (like a question or a prompt), it processes it through the layers of its neural network, predicting the most likely next word in the sequence. This process is repeated over and over, generating a coherent and meaningful response.

How Have LLMs Been Trained?

LLMs are trained using a technique called "self-supervised learning." This means they don't need humans to label the data. Instead, they learn by predicting the next word in a sentence or the next sentence in a paragraph. This training process can take weeks or even months, and it requires massive amounts of computing power.

The training data for LLMs comes from a variety of sources, including:

- **Books:** LLMs have been trained on a vast collection of books, covering various genres and topics.

- **Articles:** News articles, scientific papers, and online blogs are also used to train LLMs.
- **Websites:** LLMs have been exposed to a vast amount of text from the internet, including Wikipedia, social media posts, and online forums.
- **Code:** Code snippets and software documentation help LLMs learn the structure and logic of programming languages.
- **Images:** Some LLMs are trained on images as well, allowing them to generate captions for images or even answer questions about what's happening in a picture.

Introducing Multi-Modal Models: The Next Level of AI

While LLMs are super impressive, there's a new type of AI on the block that's even cooler: multi-modal models! These AI models can understand and process not just text, but also images, audio, and even video. They're like the ultimate multi-taskers of the AI world!

Think of it like this: A multi-modal model is like a super-smart friend who can read, write, listen to music, watch movies, and understand what's happening in a picture – all at the same time! This allows them to do even more amazing things, like:

- **Image captioning:** Describing what's happening in a picture with amazing accuracy.
- **Text-to-image generation:** Creating realistic images based on text descriptions.
- **Video understanding:** Analyzing videos to identify objects, actions, and even emotions.
- **Audio transcription:** Converting spoken language into text with high accuracy.

Vector Embeddings: The Language of Large Language Models

At the heart of large language models (LLMs) like GPT lies a fascinating concept called vector embeddings. To understand this, let's start with a simple idea: words have meaning. But how do we teach a computer about these meanings?

Vector Embeddings: Words as Coordinates

Vector embeddings are a way to represent words (or even phrases and sentences) as points in a high-dimensional space. This space isn't like our familiar 3D world; it can have hundreds or even thousands of dimensions. The position of each word in this space is determined by its relationship to other words, creating a semantic map where meaning is encoded as proximity.

The Math Behind It: Word2Vec and Beyond

One of the groundbreaking methods for creating word embeddings is called Word2Vec. It leverages neural networks to analyze vast amounts of text data, learning the statistical co-occurrence patterns of words. The result is a vector for each word, capturing its semantic essence. Other algorithms like GloVe (Global Vectors for Word Representation) have also contributed to this field, refining the way embeddings capture meaning.

Why Embeddings Matter for LLMs

Vector embeddings are crucial for large language models for several reasons:

1. **Semantic Understanding:** By representing words as vectors, LLMs can measure the semantic similarity between words using simple mathematical operations like cosine similarity. This allows them to understand analogies ("king" is to "man" as "queen" is to "woman"), identify synonyms ("happy" and "joyful"), and even reason about complex relationships between concepts.

2. **Contextual Awareness:** Embeddings are dynamic; they change based on the context. The same word can have different meanings in different sentences. For example, "bank" could refer to a financial institution or the side of a river. Modern LLMs often use transformer architectures that can generate context-specific

embeddings for words, enabling them to generate text that is both coherent and relevant to the situation.

3. **Mathematical Operations:** Embeddings allow us to perform algebraic operations on words. The famous example is "king" - "man" + "woman" ≈ "queen." This property allows LLMs to perform analogical reasoning, a hallmark of human intelligence.

4. **Dimensionality Reduction:** While word embeddings can have hundreds or thousands of dimensions, techniques like Principal Component Analysis (PCA) can be used to reduce the dimensionality while preserving most of the semantic information. This makes computations more efficient without sacrificing too much accuracy.

The Impact on Language Generation

Vector embeddings have revolutionized language generation. By understanding words in this rich, multi-dimensional way, LLMs can produce text that's not only grammatically correct but also semantically sophisticated, nuanced, and contextually relevant. They can translate between languages, summarize articles, write code, and even create poetry. In a Nutshell, Think of vector embeddings as a bridge between human language and the mathematical language that computers understand. They transform words into numerical coordinates, unlocking a world of possibilities for language understanding and generation. This is the bedrock upon which the remarkable capabilities of modern AI language models are built.

Different Flavors of LLMs and Multi-Modal Models

- **GPT (OpenAI):** Known for its creative writing abilities and conversational skills, GPT powers ChatGPT and other text generation tools.
- **LaMDA (Google):** This conversational AI is designed to engage in open-ended dialogues on a wide range of topics, showcasing a deeper understanding of context and nuance.
- **Gemini Pro (Google):** This is the advanced model from Google AI, designed to power Google Search and other Google products with its superior language understanding and generation capabilities. It's also a multi-modal model, so it can understand and process images as well as text.
- **BERT (Google):** BERT is excellent at understanding the meaning of words in context and is often used for tasks like search and language translation.
- **T5 (Google):** T5 is a versatile model that can be fine-tuned for various tasks, including translation, summarization, and question-answering.

Technical Lingo for LLM Explorers

Here are some key terms you'll encounter when exploring the world of LLMs and multi-modal models:

- **Parameters:** These are the values that an AI model learns during training. The more parameters, the more complex the model and the better it can perform on various tasks.
- **Transformer Architecture:** This is a type of neural network architecture that is particularly effective for natural language processing and multi-modal tasks. Most modern LLMs and multi-modal models use some form of Transformer architecture.
- **Prompt Engineering:** This refers to the art of crafting prompts (the text or image input you give to an AI model) to get the desired output.

Accessing LLMs and Multi-Modal Models

You can access many LLMs and multi-modal models through online platforms and APIs:

- **Google AI Platform:** Provides access to various Google AI models, including BERT, T5, LaMDA, and Gemini Pro, for different tasks.
- **OpenAI API:** Provides access to GPT models for text generation, completion, and other tasks.
- **Hugging Face Transformers Library:** Offers a wide range of pre-trained LLMs and multi-modal models, along with tools for fine-tuning them for specific applications.

Remember, LLMs and multi-modal models are still under development, and they have their limitations. But they are already transforming the way we interact with computers and the world around us.

Language Whiz Workout: Exercises for the LLM Chapter!

Get ready to train your own language superpowers with these fun and challenging LLM exercises:

1. Chatbot Challenge:

Mission: Have a conversation with a chatbot and see if you can tell it's not a human.

What to do:

- Choose a chatbot platform like Google Gemini or ChatGPT.
- Start a conversation and ask questions on various topics.
- Observe the responses and try to identify any clues that it's a bot.
- Can you trick the chatbot with tricky questions or jokes?

💡 Why it matters: This exercise helps you understand the strengths and limitations of current chatbots and appreciate how far AI has come in natural language processing.

2. **The Storyteller's Apprentice:**

Mission: Collaborate with an LLM to write a creative story.

What to do:

- Use a text generation tool like Google Gemini or ChatGPT.
- Provide a starting prompt, such as "a group of friends discover a hidden portal to another dimension."
- Let the AI generate the next part of the story.
- Continue collaborating, taking turns adding new elements to the plot.
- See how your story unfolds with the help of your AI writing partner!

💡 Why it matters: This exercise demonstrates how LLMs can be used for creative writing and storytelling, sparking your imagination and unlocking new ideas.

3. **The Detective's Dilemma:**

Mission: Use an LLM to help you solve a mystery or puzzle.

What to do:

- Choose a riddle, a logic puzzle, or even a fictional mystery.
- Ask the LLM for clues, hints, or possible solutions.

- Analyze the LLM's responses and use them to solve the puzzle.

💡 Why it matters: This exercise highlights the problem-solving capabilities of LLMs and shows how they can be used as a tool for research and discovery.

4. **Language Explorer:**

Mission: Use an LLM to learn about different languages and cultures.

What to do:

- Ask the LLM to translate phrases or sentences into different languages.
- Learn about the cultural context and significance of different words and expressions.
- Practice your language skills by having a conversation with the LLM in a foreign language.

💡 Why it matters: This exercise demonstrates the potential of LLMs to break down language barriers and foster cultural understanding.

Prompt Engineering: Whispering in AI's Ear!

Think of AI as a super-smart friend who's eager to help, but sometimes needs a little guidance to understand what you want. That's where prompt engineering comes in! It's like learning the secret language that AI understands, so you can communicate with it clearly and get the best results.

What is Prompt Engineering?

Prompt engineering is the art of crafting clear, specific instructions (prompts) that guide AI models to generate the desired output. Think of it like giving directions to a robot chef – the more detailed and precise your instructions, the more likely you are to get the dish you want!

Key Components of a Good Prompt:

1. **Instruction:** Tell the AI what you want it to do. Be

clear and direct, like "Write a poem about a dancing elephant" or "Explain photosynthesis in simple terms."

2. **Context:** Provide any necessary background information or context to help the AI understand your request. For example, if you want a poem about a specific type of elephant, mention it.

3. **Constraints:** Specify any limitations or requirements you have for the output. For example, you might want the poem to be a certain length, rhyme, or follow a particular style.

4. **Output Format:** Let the AI know what kind of response you expect. Do you want a list, a paragraph, a poem, or code?

Example of a Well-Crafted Prompt:

"Write a short poem about a playful elephant dancing in the jungle. Use vivid imagery and a rhyming scheme."

Let's break it down:

- **Instruction:** Write a short poem.
- **Context:** The poem is about a playful elephant dancing in the jungle.
- **Constraints:** Use vivid imagery and a rhyming scheme.
- **Output Format:** A poem.

By providing all this information, you're giving the AI the best chance of creating a poem that meets your expectations.

More Prompt Examples:

- **General:** "Explain the concept of gravity to a 5-year-old."
- **Specific:** "Write a persuasive essay arguing for the importance of recycling, using facts and statistics."
- **Creative:** "Imagine you're a time traveler from the year 3000. Write a journal entry about your first day in the 21st century."
- **Technical:** "Generate Python code to calculate the average of a list of numbers."

Tips for Effective Prompt Engineering:

- **Be clear and concise:** Avoid ambiguity and use precise language.
- **Think like the AI:** Consider how the AI might interpret your words and try to anticipate any misunderstandings.
- **Iterate and experiment:** Don't be afraid to try different prompts and refine them until you get the desired results.
- **Use examples:** If you have specific examples in mind, share them with the AI to guide its output.

Remember: Prompt engineering is an evolving art. As AI models get smarter, we'll learn new and better ways to communicate with them. But the key is to be patient, experiment, and have fun with it! The possibilities are endless!

A Token: A Bite-Sized Piece of Language for AI

Imagine you have a delicious pizza, and you want to share it with your friends. You cut it into slices, right? Well, AI models like to do something similar with language! They break down words and sentences into smaller chunks called tokens.

A token can be a whole word, part of a word, or even just a single character. It's like a bite-sized piece of language that AI can easily digest and understand.

1. **AI Food:** Tokens are the building blocks that AI models use to understand and generate text. They're like the ingredients in a recipe – without them, the AI can't create anything meaningful.

2. **Memory Management:** AI models have a limited amount of memory, just like your brain can only hold

so much information at once. Tokens help AI models manage their memory more efficiently by breaking down large chunks of text into smaller, more manageable pieces.

3. **Context Clues:** Tokens also help AI models understand the context of a sentence. By looking at the tokens around a word, the AI can figure out what the word means in that particular sentence.

How Many Tokens are in a Word?

The number of tokens in a word can vary depending on the language and the specific AI model. But generally, shorter words like "cat" or "dog" are usually one token, while longer words like "elephant" or "hippopotamus" might be split into multiple tokens.

For example, the word "fantastic" might be split into two tokens: "fan" and "tastic."

How Do AI Models Count Tokens?

AI models use special algorithms (like math formulas) to count tokens. These algorithms look at the text and decide how to break it down into smaller chunks. Different models have different ways of counting tokens, but the idea is the same: to make language easier for AI to understand and process.

Token Tips for Prompt Engineers

If you're playing around with AI tools like ChatGPT, it's helpful to know a little bit about tokens. Here are a few tips:

- **Shorter Prompts:** Since AI models have limited memory, shorter prompts are often easier for them to process.
- **Clear Instructions:** Using clear and concise language will help the AI understand your request better.
- **Experiment:** Try different ways of phrasing your prompts to see what gets the best results.

Fun Prompt Engineering Exercises for you!

Get ready to train your AI whispering skills with these fun and engaging exercises:

1. **The Magic Wand Prompt:** Imagine you have a magic wand that can create anything you wish. Write a prompt for an AI artist to draw your wildest creation. Remember to be specific about the colors, shapes, and details!

_____
_____
_____
_____
_____
_____

2. **Animal Adventures Prompt:** Choose your favorite animal and imagine it going on an exciting adventure. Write a prompt for an AI storyteller to write a short story about your animal's journey. Think about where it goes, who it meets, and what challenges it overcomes.

_____
_____
_____
_____
_____
_____
_____
_____

3. **Time Traveler Prompt:** Imagine you can travel back in time to meet your favorite historical figure. Write a prompt for an AI chatbot to role-play as that person and have a conversation with you. What questions would you ask? What would you want to learn from them?

_____
_____
_____
_____
_____
_____
_____
_____

4. **Songwriting Challenge:** Think of your favorite type of music (pop, rock, rap, etc.) and a topic that inspires you. Write a prompt for an AI music generator to create a catchy song about your chosen topic. Don't forget to mention the instruments you want to hear!

_____
_____
_____
_____
_____
_____
_____
_____

5. **Explain It Like I'm 5 Prompt:** Pick a complex topic like gravity, photosynthesis, or even how the internet works. Write a prompt for an AI to explain it in simple terms that a 5-year-old could understand. Use fun analogies and examples!

_____
_____
_____
_____
_____
_____
_____
_____

6. **The Emoji Story Prompt:** Choose 3-5 emojis that tell a story. Write a prompt for an AI to create a short story based on those emojis. Get creative and see what the AI comes up with!

_____
_____
_____
_____
_____
_____
_____
_____
_____

7. **Dream Invention Prompt:** What's a problem you wish you could solve with a cool invention? Write a prompt for an AI to design your dream invention. Describe what it does, how it looks, and how it helps people.

_____
_____
_____
_____
_____
_____
_____
_____
_____

Bonus Challenge:

Try giving the same prompt to different AI tools and compare the results! See how each AI interprets your instructions and what kind of unique creations they come up with.

Remember, the more specific and descriptive your prompts are, the better the AI will understand what you want. So be as creative as you can and have fun exploring the world of AI communication!

Chain-of-Thought (CoT) Prompting: Helping AI Think Step-by-Step!

Imagine trying to explain how to bake a cake to a friend who has never even seen an oven before. You wouldn't just say, "Mix the ingredients and bake!" You'd give them detailed instructions, explaining each step in order, right?

Chain-of-Thought (CoT) Prompting is like giving those step-by-step instructions to AI. It helps AI break down complex problems into smaller, easier-to-understand steps, making it smarter and more capable.

Why is CoT Prompting Important?

1. **Better Problem Solving:** AI models are great at understanding language and generating text, but sometimes they struggle with complex reasoning. CoT prompting helps them think more logically and arrive at the right answer by guiding them through a series of

thought processes. It's like giving them a map to navigate through a tricky maze!

2. **Improved Accuracy:** By breaking down problems into smaller steps, CoT prompting reduces the chances of AI making errors. This is especially important for tasks that require precise calculations or logical reasoning.

3. **Increased Transparency:** CoT prompting makes it easier for us to understand how AI arrives at its answers. By seeing the step-by-step reasoning process, we can identify any potential errors or biases and make improvements to the AI model.

4. **Enhanced Creativity:** Sometimes, the best solutions to problems come from thinking outside the box. CoT prompting can encourage AI to explore different approaches and generate more creative and innovative ideas.

How Does CoT Prompting Work?

It's actually quite simple! Instead of just asking AI a question directly, we provide it with a series of intermediate steps that lead to the final answer.

For example, instead of asking "What is the capital of France?", we could ask:

1. "What is the largest country in Western Europe?"

2. "What is the most populous city in that country?"

3. "What is the capital of that city?"

By breaking down the question into these smaller steps, we guide the AI through a chain of thought that helps it arrive at the correct answer: Paris.

CoT Prompting in Action

CoT prompting is being used in various applications:

- **Math and Science:** AI can solve complex problems by breaking them down into smaller equations or steps.
- **Reasoning and Logic:** AI can solve puzzles and riddles by following a logical chain of thought.
- **Writing and Creative Tasks:** AI can generate more coherent and creative stories or poems by planning out the plot or structure in advance.

The Future of CoT Prompting

As AI continues to evolve, CoT prompting will play an even more important role in making it smarter, more accurate, and more useful in our daily lives. It's an exciting field with endless possibilities!

So, next time you chat with an AI, remember that a little bit of guidance can go a long way! By using CoT prompting, we can help AI think more clearly, solve problems more effectively, and unlock its full potential!

Chain-of-Thought Challenge: Unleash AI's Detective Skills!

Let's put AI's thinking skills to the test and see how well it can follow a chain of thought to solve complex problems! Get ready for some brain-tickling puzzles and exercises:

1. The Mystery Box Challenge:

Mission: Help an AI model uncover what's hidden inside a mysterious box by asking a series of questions.

What to do:

- Imagine a box containing a secret object.
- Ask the AI model questions that will help you narrow down the possibilities.
- Start with broad questions like "Is it bigger than a breadbox?" or "Is it alive?"
- Gradually refine your questions based on the AI's responses.
- See how many questions it takes to figure out the mystery object!

💡 Why it matters: This exercise helps you understand how to guide AI's thinking process through a chain of logical questions and deductions.

2. The Riddler's Delight:

Mission: Use chain-of-thought prompting to help an AI model solve riddles and brain teasers.

What to do:

- Find a set of riddles or brain teasers online or in a book.
- Present the riddle to the AI model and ask it to explain its thought process as it tries to solve it.
- If the AI gets stuck, guide it with hints or ask it to elaborate on a specific step in its reasoning.
- See if you can work together to crack the code and find the answer!

💡 Why it matters: This exercise demonstrates how AI can use logical reasoning and deduction to solve complex problems.

AI Models: The Superheroes of the Digital World!

Think of AI models as superheroes with different powers. Some are super strong, some are super fast, and some are super smart. But they all have one thing in common: they're here to help us!

Types of AI Models:

Before we dive into the different types of models, it's important to understand that there are two main categories:

1. **Generic Models:** These are like all-rounders who can do a little bit of everything. They are trained on a massive amount of data from all sorts of different sources, giving them a broad understanding of language, images, and even the world around us. They're like the superheroes who can fly, shoot lasers, AND have super strength!

2. **Task-Specific Models:** These are specialists who excel at one particular task. They're trained on data that is specifically related to their area of expertise, like

medical images or financial data. They're like the superheroes who can control the weather or talk to animals - they're experts in their own special way.

How AI Models Learn: Training Time!

Think of it as teaching a puppy new tricks. You show them what to do over and over again, rewarding them when they get it right. That's kind of like how AI models learn. They're fed massive amounts of data and given feedback on their performance. This process is called training, and it's how AI models become experts at their tasks.

Now, let's meet some of the AI superheroes and their amazing superpowers:

1. **Supervised Learning Models: The Pattern Recognizers**

These models are like detectives, trained to find patterns in data. They're given examples of labeled data, like pictures of cats and dogs with the correct labels. By studying these examples, they learn to recognize the characteristics of each animal and can then classify new pictures with impressive accuracy.

- **Examples:** Image recognition (Google Photos), spam filters (Gmail), language translation (Google Translate)

2. **Unsupervised Learning Models: The Explorers**

These models are like explorers discovering hidden treasures. They're given data without any labels and tasked with finding patterns and relationships on their own. They're great at grouping similar things together (clustering) and finding outliers (anomalies).

- **Examples:** Customer segmentation (Google Analytics), anomaly detection (like fraud detection in Google Pay), recommendation systems (YouTube recommendations)

3. **Reinforcement Learning Models: The Decision-Makers**

These models are like athletes who learn by trial and error. They interact with their environment, taking actions and receiving feedback in the form of rewards or penalties. This helps them learn the best strategies to achieve their goals.

- **Examples:** Game-playing AI (like AlphaGo), robotics (controlling robot movements), self-driving cars (Waymo)

4. **Generative Models: The Creative Geniuses**

These models are like artists who can create new things from scratch. They're trained on existing data like images, music, or text and then generate new content that is similar but unique.

- **Examples:** Imagen (Google - generating images from text descriptions), MusicLM (Google - generating music from text descriptions), text-to-speech systems (Google Text-to-Speech)

5. **Large Language Models (LLMs): The Wordsmiths**

These models are like language experts who can understand and generate text that is remarkably human-like. They can be used for a wide range of tasks, from answering questions and writing essays to translating languages and even generating code.

- **Examples:** Gemini (Google), LaMDA (Google), Gemini Pro (Google), GPT, LLaMA etc

6. **Multi-Modal Models: The All-Rounders**

These models are like the superheroes who have multiple powers. They can understand and process different types of data, such as text, images, and audio. This allows them to tackle more complex tasks, like generating image descriptions or answering questions about videos.

- **Examples:** Gemini Pro (Google), Flamingo (DeepMind)

These are just a few of the many types of AI models out

there. As AI research continues to advance, we can expect to see even more amazing models with new and unexpected capabilities. It's an exciting time to be learning about AI!

Superpower Training: Exercises for the AI Models Chapter!

Hey there, budding AI trainers! Let's put your knowledge about AI models to the test and unleash their superpowers through these fun and engaging exercises!

1. Model Matchmaker:

Mission: Match the AI model with its perfect superpower!

What to do:

- Create two lists: one with different types of AI models (e.g., supervised learning, unsupervised learning, reinforcement learning, generative models) and another with different tasks or applications (e.g., image recognition, language translation, game playing, music composition).

- Draw lines connecting each AI model type to the tasks it's best suited for.

- Explain why each model is well-suited for its assigned task.

💡 Why it matters: This exercise helps you understand the strengths and weaknesses of different AI models and how to choose the right one for a specific task.

2. The Model Trainer Challenge:

Mission: Imagine you're training an AI model to become a superhero.

What to do:

- Choose a superpower you want to give your AI model (e.g., super strength, flight, invisibility).
- Describe the types of data and training you would provide to help your model develop this superpower.
- Explain how you would test and evaluate your model's performance.
- Share your training plan with others and get their feedback!

💡 Why it matters: This exercise helps you understand the process of training AI models and the importance of choosing the right data and training methods.

Model Hallucination: When AI's Imagination Runs Wild!

Imagine your AI friend is telling you a story about a flying elephant that delivers pizzas. Sounds fun, right? But there's a problem: flying elephants don't exist! This is an example of AI hallucination, where AI models make up things that aren't real or true.

What is AI Hallucination?

AI hallucination is when an AI model, like a chatbot or language model, generates information that is not supported by its training data or real-world knowledge. It's like the AI is making things up out of thin air! This can happen for several reasons:

- **Limited Knowledge**: The model hasn't been trained on enough information to understand certain topics fully.

- **Confusing Patterns**: The model might pick up on incorrect or misleading patterns in the data it has learned from.

- **Overconfidence**: Sometimes, the model might be too confident in its abilities and generate information even when it's unsure.

How to Tame the AI's Imagination: Input Parameters & Tips

While we can't completely stop AI hallucinations, there are things we can do to reduce them:

- **Training Data:** Feeding the AI model a large and diverse dataset can help it learn a broader range of information and reduce the chances of it making things up.

- **Temperature:** This parameter controls how creative the AI is. A lower temperature makes the AI more likely to stick to facts, while a higher temperature encourages more imaginative responses.

- **Top-P and Top-K Sampling:** These techniques help the AI choose from the most likely next words in a sentence, reducing the chances of it going off on a tangent.

- **Prompt Engineering:** Careful crafting of prompts (the instructions you give to the AI) can also help guide it towards more accurate and grounded responses.

Strategies adopted by large enterprises for Taming Hallucinations

Companies that use AI for customer service are always working to make their chatbots more reliable and trustworthy. Here are some strategies they use:

- **Retrieval-Augmented Generation (RAG):** This approach combines the creative power of language models with the ability to look up information from reliable sources. It's like giving the AI a cheat sheet to check its answers!

- **Human in the Loop:** Having humans review and correct the AI's responses helps to ensure accuracy and catch any hallucinations before they reach customers.

- **Continuous Feedback:** By collecting feedback from users, companies can identify areas where the AI is struggling and make improvements over time.

Grounded in Factuality

"Grounded in factuality" means that AI models prioritize generating responses that are based on reliable, verifiable information. This is especially important for language models, which are designed to generate human-like text. If an AI isn't grounded in factuality, it may "hallucinate" or make up information that is incorrect, misleading, or even harmful.

To achieve groundedness in factuality, AI models can be trained on large datasets of verified information and use techniques like retrieval-augmented generation (RAG) to access external knowledge bases for accurate answers. They can also be fine-tuned to prioritize factual accuracy and avoid making unsupported claims.

Here's why being grounded in factuality is crucial:

- **Trustworthiness**: Users are more likely to trust AI models that consistently provide accurate and reliable information.

- **Safety**: Inaccurate or misleading information from AI can have serious consequences, especially in areas like healthcare, finance, or legal advice.

- **Utility**: AI models that are grounded in factuality are more useful for tasks like answering questions, summarizing information, and generating factual reports.

Efforts to make AI more grounded in factuality are ongoing, and there are various techniques and approaches being developed to address this important issue. As AI becomes more integrated into our lives, ensuring its groundedness in factuality will be crucial for its responsible and beneficial use.

Remember, AI is still a young technology, and it's learning all the time. By understanding its limitations and working to improve it, we can create AI systems that are not only powerful but also trustworthy and reliable.

AI Hallucination Detective Training: Spot the Fake News!

1. Fact or Fiction Face-Off:

Mission: Analyze news headlines or social media posts and determine if they're real or AI-generated.

What to do:

- Gather a collection of news headlines or social media posts, some real and some potentially generated by AI.

- Carefully examine each one for clues that might indicate it's fake. Look for inconsistencies, exaggerations, or unusual phrasing.

- Use online tools like fact-checking websites or reverse image search to verify the information.

💡 Why it matters: This exercise helps you develop critical thinking skills and become a savvy consumer of information in the age of AI.

2. The AI Storyteller's Challenge (with a Twist!):

Mission: Write a story with an AI, but pay close attention to any made-up facts or details.

What to do:

- Use a text generation tool to collaborate on a story.

- Start with a prompt that includes some real-world facts or historical events.

- As the AI generates the story, watch out for any inaccuracies or inconsistencies.

- Gently correct the AI and guide it back to the facts.

💡 Why it matters: This exercise highlights the importance of human oversight in AI-generated content and helps you understand how to work with AI to produce accurate and reliable information.

AI at Work: Helping Humans Do Amazing Things!

Imagine having a super-smart assistant who can tackle your to-do list, organize your inbox, and even brainstorm creative ideas with you! That's the power of AI in today's world! Whether you're a student, artist, doctor, or entrepreneur, AI is  here to boost your productivity and unlock your full potential.

For **Artists**, AI can generate endless inspiration, suggest color palettes, or even help create entire compositions.

Chefs can get recipe ideas tailored to their ingredients, and even have AI adjust cooking times to perfection!

Business teams can analyze market trends, automate tedious tasks, and discover untapped opportunities.

Mechanics can diagnose car problems in a flash, while architects can design buildings that are both beautiful and energy-efficient.

But here's the kicker: This isn't just science fiction! AI is already making these things happen. And the best part? It's just the beginning! Imagine AI personal trainers who create custom workouts based on your goals and fitness levels, or AI language tutors who make learning new languages fun and effortless. The possibilities are endless!

Remember, though, AI is a tool, not a magic wand. It's up to us humans to harness its power and use it wisely. So let's dream big, work together, and create an AI-powered future that's even more awesome than we can imagine!

Disclaimer: While these ideas are based on current AI capabilities, some applications might still be in development and not yet widely available. But who knows, maybe you'll be the one to create them!

AI is Everywhere, Making Things Awesome!

Here's how AI is already working behind the scenes to make your favorite apps and websites super cool and helpful:

Google Search: The Mind-Reading Search Engine

- **How it helps you:** Ever noticed how Google seems to know exactly what you're looking for? That's AI at work! It looks at what you've searched for before, what other people search for, and even understands the meaning behind your words. This  helps Google show you the most relevant and helpful results, making it easier than ever to find what you need. AI also powers Google's ability to answer your questions directly or provide quick facts right in the search results, saving you time and effort.

YouTube: Your Personalized Video Playlist

- **How it helps you:** Do you ever feel like YouTube knows exactly what videos you want to watch? That's AI again! It analyzes your watch history, likes, and dislikes to create a personalized video feed just for you. It also helps with subtitles, automatic video recommendations, and even identifying harmful or inappropriate content.

Spotify and Apple Music: The DJs That Know Your Taste

- **How it helps you**: AI-powered music streaming services like Spotify and Apple Music are like having a personal DJ who knows exactly what you want to hear. They analyze your listening habits and create playlists tailored to your mood, activity, or even the time of day. They also suggest new songs and artists you might like, helping you discover your next favorite jam.

Netflix and Other Streaming Services: The Movie Matchmakers

- **How it helps you**: Ever wondered how Netflix seems to always suggest the almost perfect movie for you? It's all thanks to AI! By analyzing your viewing history, ratings, and even the time of day you watch, AI can predict what you'll enjoy next. This makes movie night a breeze, as you don't have to scroll through endless titles to find something you'll like.

Google Maps: Your Personal Navigator

- **How it helps you**: AI makes Google Maps more than just a map. It analyzes real-time traffic data to help you find the fastest route, predicts your arrival time accurately, and even suggests places you might like based on your past searches and interests. It's like having a super-smart co-pilot who always knows the way!

Robot Helpers: Your Smartest Sidekick

- **How it helps you:** While we don't have robot butlers quite yet, AI-powered robots are already helping us in many ways. In factories, robots use AI to assemble products quickly and accurately. In homes, robot vacuums use AI to map out your house and clean efficiently. And in some restaurants, robot waiters are even serving up your food!

AI Doctors: The Medical Marvels

- **How it helps you:** AI is transforming healthcare! It can help doctors diagnose diseases more accurately by analyzing medical images and patient data. AI can also personalize treatment plans, predict patient outcomes, and even discover new drugs. It's like having a super-smart doctor on your healthcare team!

Creative Artists: The AI-Powered Picassos

- **How it helps you:** AI isn't just about science and technology - it's also revolutionizing the world of art! AI artists can create stunning paintings, sculptures, and even music that is indistinguishable from human-created works. They can also generate unique designs and patterns for fashion, architecture, and other creative fields.

Social Media: The Friend Finder and Filter

- **How it helps you**: AI is working hard to make your social media experience better in many ways. It helps you connect with friends and family by suggesting people you might know, filtering out spam and fake news, and even generating automatic captions for your photos and videos.

Shopping Online: The Personal Shopper

- **How it helps you**: Have you ever noticed how online stores recommend products that seem to be exactly what you were looking for? That's AI at play! It analyzes your browsing and purchase history to suggest items you might like, and even shows you personalized deals and discounts.

Email: The Inbox Organizer

- **How it helps you**: Tired of sorting through endless emails? AI is here to help! It can filter out spam, prioritize important messages, and even suggest quick replies to save you time. Some email services even use AI to generate personalized email templates for you, making communication a breeze.

These are just a few of the many ways AI is already making our lives easier and more fun. It's like having a team of super-smart helpers working behind the scenes to make our world more exciting and efficient!

AI at Work Challenge: Become an AI Detective!

AI is already hard at work, making our lives easier, safer, and more efficient in countless ways. Let's go on a mission to discover how AI is transforming the way we work and play!

1. AI in Everyday Jobs Scavenger Hunt:

Mission: Uncover the hidden AI helpers in different professions.

What to do:

- Interview people you know about their jobs. Ask them if they use any tools or software that seem "smart" or automated.

- Research different industries like healthcare, transportation, manufacturing, and entertainment. Look for examples of how AI is used to automate tasks, make decisions, or improve efficiency.

- Create a list or a presentation of your findings, highlighting the most interesting and surprising examples of AI at work.

💡 Why it matters: This helps you understand how AI is already impacting various professions and the potential it has to transform the way we work.

2. Design Your Own AI-Powered Workplace:

Mission: Imagine a workplace where AI and humans work together seamlessly.

What to do:

- Think about your dream job or a profession you're interested in.

- Brainstorm ways AI could be used to improve that workplace, automate tasks, or enhance productivity.

- Present your vision to your friends or family and get their feedback.

💡 Why it matters: This exercise encourages you to think creatively about how AI can be used to solve problems and create more efficient and enjoyable work environments.

AI and Us: Being Friends with Robots

Fair Play for AI: Teaching Robots to be Kind and Fair

Imagine a playground where everyone gets a turn on the swings, no matter who they are. That's what we want for AI too! But teaching Artificial Intelligence (AI) to be kind and fair is a bit trickier than teaching kids to share. Let's explore why it's important and how we can make AI play nice.

Why Fairness Matters in AI

Just like people, AI can learn biases from the information it's trained on. This means it might make unfair decisions, like recommending a job to someone based on their gender or ethnicity instead of their skills. That's not cool, right? We want AI to treat everyone equally and give everyone a fair chance.

Unfair AI can lead to all sorts of problems:

- **Discrimination:** AI could unfairly judge people and deny them opportunities they deserve.

- **Inequality:** AI could make the rich richer and the poor poorer by giving them different treatment.

- **Mistrust:** If people don't trust AI, they won't use it, and we'll miss out on all the good things it can do.

Teaching AI to Play Fair

Teaching AI to be kind and fair is a big challenge, but lots of smart people are working on it. Here's how:

1. **Data Detox:** AI learns from massive amounts of data, but this data can be biased. To teach AI fairness, we need to make sure the data it learns from is diverse and representative of everyone. It's like making sure the AI eats a healthy diet of information!

2. **Algorithm Checkup:** Algorithms are the instructions that tell AI how to make decisions. We need to check these algorithms for any hidden biases that might lead to unfair outcomes. It's like giving AI a regular health check-up to make sure everything is working properly.

3. **Transparency Time:** We need to know how AI makes decisions so we can spot any unfairness. It's like asking AI to show its work on a math problem so we can see how it got the answer.

4. **Human Helpers:** Even the smartest AI needs a helping hand sometimes. Humans should be involved in checking AI's decisions and making sure it's not doing anything unethical. It's like having a referee on the playground to keep things fair.

Real-World Examples: Fair Play in Action

- **Fairer Lending:** Some banks use AI to decide who gets a loan, but this can be biased. New AI systems are being developed to assess creditworthiness based on a wider range of factors, making it fairer for everyone.

- **Unbiased Hiring:** AI can help companies find the best candidates for jobs, but it can also pick up on biases in resumes and interviews. Companies are now working to make AI hiring tools more fair and objective.

- **Inclusive Education:** AI-powered tutoring systems can help students learn at their own pace, but they need to be designed to support learners of all backgrounds and abilities.

- **Equal Access to Healthcare:** AI can help doctors diagnose diseases and recommend treatments, but it needs to be accessible to everyone, regardless of their location or socioeconomic status.

What you Can Do to Help

You might be wondering, "What can I do to make AI fair?" Well, even though you're not a scientist (yet!), there are things you can do:

- **Ask Questions:** When you see AI in action, ask questions about how it works and if it's fair. This helps to raise awareness and encourage companies to make AI more transparent.

- **Be a Critical Thinker:** Don't just believe everything you see or hear from AI. Check the source and try to find other information to confirm what you've learned.

- **Learn About AI:** The more you know about AI, the better equipped you'll be to understand its impact on the world and advocate for fair and ethical use.

The Future of Fair AI

By working together, we can create a future where AI is a force for good, helping us solve problems and make the world a better place for everyone. It's like creating a playground where all kids can play together, no matter who they are or where they come from.

Remember, teaching AI to be kind and fair is an ongoing process, but it's a crucial one. By taking steps to ensure fairness in AI, we're not just building better technology, we're building a better future for all.

AI and Us: Becoming Best Buds with Robots

Calling all curious minds! AI isn't just about super-smart computers; it's about building relationships with amazing machines. Let's dive into how AI is becoming our friend and explore the exciting possibilities of this friendship!

1. AI Empathy Exercise:

Mission: Understand how AI can show empathy.

What to do:

- Watch a video or read a story about an AI chatbot or virtual assistant that helps people.
- Pay attention to how the AI responds to emotions and provides support.
- Discuss with friends or family how AI can be programmed to understand and respond to our feelings.
- Think about ways AI could be used to help people who are lonely, sad, or in need of emotional support.

💡 Why it matters: This helps you understand that AI isn't just about logic and reasoning – it can also be designed to recognize and respond to emotions, making it a valuable companion and support system.

2. The Ethics of AI Friendships:

Mission: Discuss the ethical considerations of forming close relationships with AI.

What to do:

- Read articles or watch videos about AI companions and chatbots.
- Discuss with friends or family whether it's ethical to form emotional bonds with AI.
- Consider the potential benefits and risks of AI companions, such as the potential for isolation or manipulation.
- Think about how we can ensure that AI is used ethically in developing companions and robots.

💡 Why it matters: This helps you develop critical thinking skills and understand the complex ethical issues surrounding AI and its impact on our relationships and society.

AI & Jobs: Will AI Steal Our Jobs?

Imagine a world where robots do all the work! They cook our food, drive our cars, build our houses, and even take care of our pets. Sounds like a dream, right? But wait, what about our jobs? Will there be anything left for humans to do?

AI / Robots: Super Strong, Super Fast, Super Efficient!

Robots are awesome! They're stronger and faster than humans, and they don't get tired or make mistakes (usually!). This makes them perfect for doing repetitive or dangerous tasks that humans don't want to do.

- **In Factories:** Robots are already assembling cars, electronics, and other products. They can work faster and more precisely than humans, making production cheaper and more efficient.
- **In Warehouses:** Robots are helping to pick, pack, and ship packages. They can lift heavy boxes and work 24/7 without needing breaks.

- **In Hospitals:** Robots are assisting surgeons in delicate operations, delivering medications, and even disinfecting rooms to keep patients safe.
- **On Farms:** Robots are milking cows, picking fruits and vegetables, and even weeding fields, freeing up farmers to focus on other tasks.

But Will AI Take ALL the Jobs?

It's true that AI is getting better at doing many jobs that were once done by humans. But don't worry, they won't take *all* the jobs! In fact, they might even create new ones.

- **New Jobs for Robot Teachers:** Someone needs to design, build, program, and maintain these robots. That means there will be lots of new jobs for engineers, technicians, and other skilled workers.
- **Jobs for Creative Thinkers:** Robots are good at following instructions, but they're not very good at creative thinking (Yet) or solving complex problems. That's where humans come in! We'll still be needed to come up with new ideas, design new products, and find innovative solutions to challenges.
- **Jobs for Caregivers:** Robots might be able to perform physical tasks, but they can't replace human empathy

and compassion. There will always be a need for people in healthcare, education, and other fields where human connection is important.

Working Together: A AI-Human Team!

The future of work is likely to be a collaboration between humans and robots. Robots will handle the repetitive and dangerous tasks, freeing up humans to focus on what we do best: being creative, solving problems, and caring for others. It's like having a super-powered sidekick who can help us do our jobs better and achieve more!

Our AI Future Challenge: Designing a World Where AI Works for Everyone!

1. The AI Superhero Squad:

Mission: Assemble a team of AI-powered superheroes to tackle the world's biggest problems.

What to do:

- Brainstorm a list of global challenges, such as climate change, disease, poverty, or inequality.
- Create a team of AI superheroes with unique powers tailored to address each problem. Describe their special abilities and how they use AI to make a difference.
- Draw pictures or write stories about your AI superheroes in action, saving the day and making the world a better place.

💡 Why it matters: This exercise sparks your imagination and helps you think about how AI can be used to solve real-world problems and create positive change.

2. The Sustainable City of the Future:

Mission: Design a city where AI technology helps create a sustainable and eco-friendly environment.

What to do:

- Imagine a city where AI optimizes energy usage, manages waste, and promotes green transportation.
- Draw a map of your city, highlighting its AI-powered features like smart grids, self-driving public transport, and vertical farms.
- Write a description of your city, explaining how AI makes it a sustainable and livable place for everyone.

💡 Why it matters: This exercise encourages you to think about how AI can be used to create a more sustainable future for our planet and its inhabitants.

Our AI Future: Let's Build an Awesome World Together!

Buckle up, because we're about to blast off into the future! AI isn't just a cool gadget or a helpful tool – it's a chance for us to create a world that's even more amazing than the one we live in now. But here's the secret: we need to build this future together!

AI Heroes: AI to the Rescue!

AI has the potential to tackle some of the biggest problems facing our planet. It's like having a team of super-smart scientists, engineers, and inventors working tirelessly to find solutions.

- **Climate Change Fighters:** AI can analyze massive amounts of climate data, helping us understand how our planet is changing and predict future trends. It can also help us develop cleaner energy sources, optimize our energy use, and even create new technologies to remove carbon dioxide from the atmosphere.
- **Sustainability Superstars:** AI can optimize production processes, reduce waste, and help us create a more circular economy where resources are reused and recycled. It can even monitor deforestation and illegal fishing to protect our planet's precious ecosystems.

- **Food Waste Warriors:** AI can optimize food supply chains, predict demand, and even create personalized meal plans to reduce food waste at home and in businesses. It can also help us develop new ways to grow food more sustainably, using less water and fewer resources.

Building a Better World: AI for Everyone!

Imagine a world where everyone has access to clean water, nutritious food, affordable healthcare, and quality education. AI can help us make this a reality by:

- **Personalized Learning:** AI-powered tutors can adapt to each student's learning style, helping them reach their full potential.
- **Accessible Healthcare:** AI can help doctors diagnose diseases more accurately and develop personalized treatment plans, even in remote areas.
- **Clean Water Solutions:** AI can monitor water quality, predict contamination, and optimize water distribution systems to ensure everyone has access to clean water.
- **Sustainable Agriculture:** AI can help farmers improve crop yields, reduce water usage, and protect crops from pests and diseases, ensuring we have enough food to feed the growing population.

The Future is Ours to Create!

We're at a crossroads, and AI gives us the chance to choose a path towards a brighter future. By embracing this amazing technology and working together, we can create a world that's smarter, fairer, more sustainable, and full of possibilities.

Remember, AI is just a tool. It's up to us to decide how we use it. So let's use our creativity, our compassion, and our collective intelligence to build a future where AI works for the good of all humanity and our planet.

The future isn't something that just happens to us. It's something we create. And with AI by our side, we can create a future that's truly awesome!

Disclaimer: Some of these ideas are still in development and may not be available everywhere yet. But with continued research and innovation, they have the potential to become a reality. So let's dream big and work together to make the most of this incredible technology!

Your AI Adventure Begins: How to Become an AI Explorer!

Feeling inspired to dive into the amazing world of AI? Great news! There are tons of exciting ways to start learning and exploring this awesome technology. Whether you're a curious kid or a grown-up who wants to learn new tricks, here are some steps you can take to embark on your AI adventure:

1. **Spark Your Curiosity**: Start by asking questions! Why is AI so cool? How does it work? What can it do? Talk to your colleagues, mentors, or friends about AI. Watch videos, read articles, or listen to podcasts about AI. The more you learn, the more excited you'll become about all the possibilities!

2. **Dive into Books and Websites**: There are tons of amazing resources out there to help you learn about AI. Look for books, websites, and online courses designed for beginners. Start with the basics and gradually work your way up to more advanced topics. Remember, learning should be fun, so choose resources

that are engaging and easy to understand!

3. **Play with AI Tools**: The best way to learn is by doing! Experiment with different AI tools and platforms. Try generating images from text descriptions using DALL-E 2, chat with a chatbot like Google Gemini, or even build a simple AI model using tools like Teachable Machine. Don't be afraid to get creative and see what you can create!

4. **Learn the Lingo**: AI has its own special vocabulary, just like any other field. Learning key terms like "machine learning," "neural networks," and "algorithms" will help you understand how AI works and communicate with other AI enthusiasts. You can find glossaries and dictionaries of AI terms online or in books about AI.

5. **Join the Community**: There's a whole community of people who are passionate about AI! Join online forums, attend AI workshops or events, or even start your own AI club with your friends. Sharing ideas and learning from others is a great way to stay motivated and discover new things about AI.

6. **Participate in Challenges** and Competitions: Many organizations host AI challenges and competitions for students of all ages. These events give you a chance to apply your AI knowledge to real-world problems, learn from experts, and even win prizes!

7. **Keep Learning** and Exploring: AI is a constantly evolving field, so there's always something new to learn. Stay curious, keep exploring, and don't be afraid to experiment. Who knows, you might even discover the next big breakthrough in AI!

Remember, learning about AI is a journey, not a race. Take your time, have fun, and don't be discouraged if things seem difficult at first. With a little effort and a lot of curiosity, you can become an AI explorer and unlock the amazing potential of this incredible technology!

Embrace AI and experiment with the future !

- **Goal:** Learn the basics of what AI is, why it's exciting, and how it's already part of your everyday life.

- **Activities:**

    - Talk to Siri, Alexa, or Google Assistant. Ask them questions, tell them jokes, or even ask them to tell you a story!
    - Play a game against the computer. Try chess, checkers, or even a video game like Minecraft. Notice how the computer makes decisions and learns as you play.
    - Watch videos about AI. Check out fun and educational videos on YouTube Kids or other safe platforms that explain AI in simple terms.

- **Resources:**

    - Books: "Hello Ruby: Adventures in Coding" by Linda Liukas, "Artificial Intelligence for Babies" by Chris Ferrie
    - Websites: Code.org (AI for Oceans activity), Scratch (create interactive stories with AI)

The Building Blocks of AI

- **Goal:** Understand the basic concepts behind AI, like data, algorithms, and machine learning.

- **Activities:**

    - Sort objects into different categories. This helps you understand how AI models classify information.
    - Play with online machine learning demos. Some websites let you train simple AI models to recognize patterns or make predictions.
    - Build a simple chatbot. You can use online tools to create a chatbot that can answer basic questions or tell jokes.

- **Resources:**

    - Books: "Machine Learning for Kids" by Dale Lane, "How to be a Coder" by Max Waine
    - Websites: Machine Learning for Kids website, Google's Teachable Machine

AI in Action

- **Goal:** Explore the amazing things AI can do in different fields like healthcare, transportation, and entertainment.

- **Activities:**

  - Research self-driving cars. Learn how they use AI to navigate and make decisions.
  - Explore AI-powered art and music. Check out websites that generate art or music using AI.
  - Visit a science museum or technology exhibit. See how AI is being used in robots, virtual reality, and other cool technologies.

- **Resources:**

  - Books: "AI Superpowers: China, Silicon Valley, and the New World Order" by Kai-Fu Lee, "The Wild Robot" by Peter Brown (a fictional story about a robot who learns to survive)
  - Websites: AI for Good website, MIT Media Lab (Scratch projects with AI)

Building Your Own AI Skills

- **Goal:** Start learning the skills you'll need to create your own AI projects in the future.

- **Activities:**

    - Learn to code! Start with simple coding languages like Scratch or Python. There are many free online resources and tutorials.
    - Experiment with AI tools and platforms. Try out online AI tools like Google's Teachable Machine or OpenAI's GPT-3 playground.
    - Participate in AI competitions or hackathons. This can be a fun way to learn new skills and collaborate with other kids interested in AI.

- **Resources:**

    - Books: "Python for Kids" by Jason Matuszewski, "Coding for Kids: Python" by Greg Walters
    - Websites: Khan Academy (coding courses), Codecademy (Python tutorials)

Awesome Careers of the Future: Where AI is Your Superpowered Sidekick!

Not everyone wants to be a coder, and that's okay! AI is changing the game in so many different fields, even for professions you might not expect. Get ready to explore some exciting careers where AI will be your awesome sidekick, helping you achieve amazing things!

Medical Marvels: Where AI Meets Medicine!

- **Doctors and Nurses:** AI-powered tools will help doctors analyze medical images, predict diseases earlier, and even personalize treatment plans for each patient. Nurses might use AI assistants to monitor patients remotely and alert them to potential problems.

Creative Crusaders: Where AI Sparks Imagination!

- **Artists and Designers:** AI can generate new ideas and designs, collaborate on creative projects, and even create entire works of art on its own.

- **Musicians and Composers:** AI can analyze music trends, create original compositions, and even help musicians experiment with new sounds and styles.

- **Writers and Storytellers:** AI can generate story ideas, help writers overcome writer's block, and even create entire drafts of stories or scripts.

Environmental Champions: Where AI Protects Our Planet!

- **Scientists and Researchers:** AI can analyze massive amounts of environmental data to help us understand climate change, predict natural disasters, and develop sustainable solutions for a healthier planet.

- **Conservationists and Wildlife Experts:** AI-powered drones and cameras can monitor wildlife populations, track endangered species, and help us protect biodiversity.

Business Boosters: Where AI Drives Success!

- **Marketing and Sales Professionals:** AI can personalize marketing campaigns, predict customer behavior, and even automate sales processes, making businesses more efficient and profitable.

- **Financial Analysts:** AI can analyze market trends, predict stock prices, and manage investment portfolios, helping investors make smarter decisions.

Teacher Titans: Where AI Transforms Education!

- **Teachers and Educators:** AI-powered tools can personalize learning experiences for each student, provide instant feedback, and even create interactive lessons that are fun and engaging.

Exploring the Unknown: Where AI Powers Discovery!

- **Astronauts and Space Explorers:** AI can analyze data from telescopes and spacecraft, help plan missions to other planets, and even design robots that can explore the vastness of space.

- **Archaeologists and Historians:** AI can help analyze ancient texts, artifacts, and even satellite imagery to uncover hidden civilizations and rewrite history.

And the list goes on and on! The possibilities are truly endless, so keep exploring, dreaming big, and remember that AI can be your superpower in any career you choose.

Remember: While AI can be a powerful tool, it's important to develop your own skills and knowledge, too. AI is your sidekick, not your replacement! The best teams are made of humans and AI working together to achieve incredible things.

AI: Awesome... But Be Careful!

AI is like a super-smart friend, but it's important to remember that even the best friends can sometimes make mistakes. Just like anything else, AI has a dark side that we need to be aware of.

Scary Robots and Fake News:

- **Tricky Robots:** Sometimes, AI can be fooled into making mistakes. Clever tricksters can create pictures or videos that look real, but they're actually fake. These are called "deepfakes," and they can be used to spread misinformation or even trick people into believing things that aren't true.

- **Biased Robots:** AI learns from data, which is information created by humans. If this data is biased (unfair or discriminatory), then the AI might learn to be biased too! It might make decisions that aren't fair or treat people differently based on their race, gender, or other characteristics.

- **Sneaky Robots:** Some AI is designed to track what

we do online, collecting our information without our permission. This can be used for advertising or even to steal our personal information.

Be a Smart AI Explorer: Know the Risks and Stay Safe!

- **Don't Believe Everything You See:** Just because something looks real doesn't mean it is. Be skeptical of pictures and videos you see online, and check the source to make sure it's trustworthy.

- **Question Everything:** When using AI tools, ask yourself: "Where did this information come from? Is it reliable? Could there be any bias in this decision?"

- **Protect Your Privacy:** Be careful what information you share online. Use strong passwords, be wary of suspicious emails or links, and read privacy policies before using any online service.

- **Learn About AI:** The more you know about AI, the better equipped you'll be to understand its limitations and potential risks.

Superhero Companies Fighting for AI Safety!

Many companies are working hard to make AI safer and more trustworthy. Here are some of the cool things they're doing:

- **Fairness Testing:** Companies test their AI models to make sure they're fair and don't discriminate against any group of people.

- **Explainable AI:** Companies are developing ways to explain how AI makes decisions, so we can understand its reasoning and spot potential biases.

- **Human Oversight:** Companies are putting humans in the loop to check AI's work and make sure it's doing things right.

- **Transparency:** Companies are being more open about how they use AI and what data they collect, so we can make informed decisions.

Remember: AI is still a young technology, and we're all learning how to use it responsibly. By being aware of the risks, asking questions, and using AI wisely, we can ensure that it becomes a truly awesome force for good in the world!

AI All-Stars: Meet the Companies and Tech Shaping the Future!

Just like superheroes have awesome gadgets and superpowers, AI has its own set of cool tools and amazing companies that are shaping our world. Let's meet some of the AI All-Stars and see what incredible things they're up to!

ALL STAR TECH COMPAINIES

1. **Google AI/DeepMind: The Brains Behind the Operation**

- **What They Do:** Google AI focuses on making AI accessible and useful for everyone. DeepMind, a Google-owned research lab, pushes the boundaries of AI research, tackling grand challenges like protein folding and energy efficiency.

- **Cool Inventions:** Google Assistant (your helpful voice-activated friend), Waymo (self-driving cars), Gemini Pro (a powerful AI model), AlphaFold (predicting protein structures), AlphaZero (mastering games like chess and Go).

2. **Alphabet X: The Moonshot Factory**

- **What They Do:** This is Google's "moonshot factory," a place where they cook up ambitious projects that sound like they're straight out of science fiction! They're tackling big problems like climate change, renewable energy, and even making the internet available to everyone through balloons!

- **Cool Inventions:** Waymo (self-driving cars), Wing (drone delivery), , Everyday Robot (household chore robots).

3. **Meta AI: The Social Network Supercharger**

- **What They Do:** Meta AI (formerly Facebook AI) focuses on making AI that connects people, understands language, and creates amazing experiences. They're working on everything from translating languages to detecting harmful content to building the metaverse.

- **Cool Inventions:** Make-A-Scene (an AI tool that turns sketches into art), BlenderBot (a chatbot that can chat about almost anything), No Language Left Behind (a project to translate hundreds of languages), Llama 2 (open-source large language model).

4. **Microsoft: The Tech Giant with a Vision for AI**

- **What They Do:** Microsoft is integrating AI into many of its products, from Bing search to Microsoft 365 productivity tools. They are also developing AI solutions for businesses and healthcare.

- **Cool Inventions:** GitHub Copilot (an AI-powered coding assistant), Seeing AI (an app that helps visually impaired people).

5. **NVIDIA: The Powerhouse Behind AI's Muscles**

- **What They Do:** NVIDIA is the king of GPUs (Graphics Processing Units), which are like supercharged engines for AI. These chips are used to train AI models, power self-driving cars, and even create realistic video game graphics.

- **Cool Inventions:** GeForce RTX GPUs (for gamers and creators), NVIDIA Drive (for autonomous vehicles), NVIDIA Clara (for healthcare).

6. **OpenAI: The Playground of Language Wizards**

- **What They Do:** OpenAI is a research lab that focuses on developing safe and beneficial AI that can benefit all of humanity. They're known for creating ChatGPT, a powerful AI chatbot that can answer questions, write stories, and even code.

- **Cool Inventions:** ChatGPT, DALL-E (an AI that creates images from text), Whisper (an AI that transcribes speech to text).

7. **Amazon: The Online Store with an AI Secret Weapon**

- **What They Do:** Amazon uses AI to power its vast online store, helping you find the products you want and recommending new things you might like. They also have AI that powers their warehouses, helping robots pick and pack orders super fast!

- **Cool Inventions:** Alexa (a smart voice assistant), Amazon Rekognition (image and video analysis), Amazon Personalize (product recommendations), Astro (a household robot).

8. **Tesla: The Electric Car Innovator with a Robotic Soul**

- **What They Do:** Tesla is famous for its electric cars, but they're also using AI to make self-driving cars a reality. Their cars are equipped with sensors and cameras that help them understand the world around them and navigate safely.

- **Cool Inventions:** Tesla Autopilot (self-driving technology), Tesla Bot (a humanoid robot in development).

9. **IBM: The Tech Giant with a Watson for AI**

- **What They Do:** IBM has been a leader in AI for decades. Their Watson AI system is used in various fields like healthcare, finance, and customer service to analyze data, answer questions, and make predictions.

- **Cool Inventions:** Watson Health (for diagnosing diseases and personalizing treatment), Watson Assistant (a chatbot for businesses), Project Debater (an AI that can debate complex topics).

This is just a small taste of the many incredible companies and researchers working on AI. It's an exciting time to be following this field, as new breakthroughs are happening all the time. Who knows what amazing AI inventions we'll see in the coming years!

AI Superpowers in Action: Real-Life Magic!

Get ready to be amazed! AI isn't just about robots and futuristic dreams anymore. It's right here, right now, making our world more awesome in ways you might not even realize. Let's explore some of the coolest uses of AI that are happening now!

AI Artists: Painting with Pixels!

Imagine a computer that can create incredible paintings, just like a real artist! AI-powered art generators can turn your words into stunning masterpieces, mixing colors and shapes in ways you might never have imagined. Some AI artists can even imitate famous painting styles or create completely new ones. It's like having a personal art genie at your fingertips!

AI Drivers: Cruising into the Future!

Ever dreamed of having a car that drives itself? That dream is becoming a reality with self-driving cars! These futuristic vehicles use AI to navigate roads, avoid traffic jams, and even park themselves. They use cameras, sensors, and powerful computers to "see" the world around them and make smart decisions, keeping everyone safe on the road.

AI Helpers in Hospitals: Your Health's Best Friend!

AI isn't just for fun – it's also helping doctors and nurses save lives! AI-powered tools can analyze medical images (like X-rays and scans) faster and more accurately than humans, helping to spot diseases early when they're easier to treat. AI can also help doctors develop personalized treatment plans for each patient, making healthcare more effective than ever before.

AI Translators: Bridging the Language Gap!

Have you ever wanted to talk to someone from another country, but didn't speak their language? AI-powered translators are like magic wands that can instantly translate spoken or written words into different languages. This amazing technology can help people from all over the world communicate and understand each other, making our world a more connected place.

AI Scientists: Exploring the Unknown!

AI isn't just for robots and computers – it's also helping scientists make amazing discoveries! AI can analyze massive amounts of data from experiments, telescopes, and even the depths of the ocean, helping us unlock the secrets of our universe and find new ways to solve problems like climate change and disease.

And that's not all! AI is being used in so many other areas, from creating personalized news feeds and shopping recommendations to helping farmers grow more food and protecting endangered species.

Open-Source AI: The Power of Sharing for Smart Adventures!

Open-source models, in the context of AI, refer to models whose underlying code, architecture, and sometimes even the training data are made freely available to the public. This means anyone can inspect, modify, use, and redistribute the model without any licensing restrictions.

Here's what's typically open-sourced in an AI model:

- **Model Architecture**: The blueprint of the model, detailing how its components (like layers and neurons in a neural network) are connected and interact.
- **Model Weights**: The numerical parameters that the model learns during training, representing its knowledge and understanding of the data.
- **Training Code**: The code used to train the model, including the algorithms and procedures followed.
- **Inference Code**: The code used to make predictions or generate outputs using the trained model.

- **Documentation**: Detailed explanations of the model's architecture, training process, and how to use it effectively.

- **Training Data** (Sometimes): In some cases, the datasets used to train the model are also made available. This can be particularly valuable for research and transparency.

How Open-Source Models Work

1. **Release**: The creators of an open-source model make its code and other components publicly accessible, usually on platforms like GitHub.

2. **Community** Contributions: Researchers, developers, and enthusiasts from around the world can access the model, experiment with it, find and fix bugs, improve its performance, and even create new applications based on it.

3. **Collaboration and Innovation**: Open-source models foster collaboration and accelerate innovation. The collective efforts of the community lead to faster advancements and a wider range of applications for the technology.

4. **Transparency and Trust**: Open-source models promote transparency, as anyone can inspect the code and understand how the model works. This builds trust in

the technology and allows for better scrutiny of potential biases or limitations.

Benefits of Open-Source Models

- **Accessibility**: Open-source models democratize AI, making it accessible to individuals, startups, and smaller organizations who might not have the resources to develop their own models from scratch.
- **Collaboration**: They foster a collaborative environment where people can share knowledge, build upon each other's work, and collectively advance the field of AI.
- **Innovation**: Open-source models accelerate innovation by allowing anyone to experiment, modify, and build new applications on top of existing models.
- **Customization**: Users can tailor open-source models to their specific needs and use cases, leading to more effective and relevant AI solutions.

Examples of Open-Source AI Models

- Stable Diffusion: A popular open-source text-to-image model that allows users to generate images from text descriptions.
- BERT: A transformer-based language model developed by Google, used for a wide range of natural language processing tasks.
- GPT-Neo: An open-source alternative to OpenAI's GPT models, designed for text generation and other

language-based tasks.

Overall, open-source AI models are a powerful force for good, enabling wider access to AI technology, fostering collaboration, and driving innovation in the field.

Supercharged Mini-Dictionary of Awesome AI Words

1. **Algorithm:** Think of this like a recipe for a robot. It's a set of instructions that tell a computer how to solve a problem, step by step.

2. **Artificial Intelligence (AI):** This is like giving super-brains to computers! They can learn, solve problems, and even be creative. It's like having a super-smart friend who can do almost anything!

3. **Chatbot:** Have you ever chatted with a robot online? That's a chatbot! It's a computer program designed to talk to people and help them with things.

4. **Data:** This is like food for computers! Data is information that helps computers learn and understand the world. It can be anything like pictures, words, numbers, or even sounds.

5. **Deep Learning:** This is like giving a computer a su-

per-powered brain! It's a type of AI that uses many layers of artificial neurons (like tiny brain cells) to learn from massive amounts of data. It's how computers can do amazing things like recognize faces or even drive cars!

6. **Generative AI:** This is like having a robot artist or writer! Generative AI can create new things like images, text, music, or even code. It learns from existing examples and then makes something totally new.

7. **Large Language Model (LLM):** This is a super-smart language whiz! It's a type of AI model that can understand and generate human-like text. It powers chatbots, writing assistants, and even translation tools. Imagine having a friend who knows every language in the world!

8. **Machine Learning (ML):** This is like teaching a computer to learn without giving it all the answers. It figures things out by finding patterns in data, just like a detective!

9. **Model:** Think of this as a super-smart expert in a specific area. It's a computer program that's been trained on tons of data to do a specific task, like recognizing pictures of cats or translating languages.

10. **Natural Language Processing (NLP):** This is how computers understand and use human language. It's like giving computers the ability to read, write, and

even tell jokes!

11. **Neural Network:** This is like a digital brain! It's a computer program modeled after the human brain, with lots of interconnected "neurons" that help it learn.

12. **RAG (Retrieval-Augmented Generation):** This is a type of LLM that can look up information in a database to give you even smarter answers! Imagine having a chatbot that has access to the entire internet!

13. **Training Data:** This is the information used to teach a computer program. It's like showing a robot pictures of different animals so it can learn to recognize them.

14. **Whitepapers:** These are like instruction manuals for AI! They're technical documents written by researchers to explain how they built or improved an AI model. It's like getting a sneak peek behind the curtain of the AI world!

Bonus Word:

15. **Transformer:** This is a type of neural network that's especially good at understanding language. It's like the secret sauce in many LLMs, helping them to understand complex sentences and generate human-like text.

See you in the next adventure !